Publishing an Academ

Tips, Tricks, and Ta

Beth L. Hewett & Robbin Z. Warner

June 2021

Second Edition, Revised

Good Words Publishing

In cooperation with Defend & Publishing, LLC

www.defendandpublish.com

Original Copyright 2017 by Beth L. Hewett and Robbin Z. Warner

Copyright 2021, 2nd edition, revised by Beth L. Hewett and Robbin Z. Warner

No part of this publication may be reproduced, stored in a retrieval system, or transmitted in any form or by any means, electronic, mechanical, photocopying, recording, scanning, or otherwise, except as permitted under Sections 107 or 108 of the 1976 Copyright Act, without either the prior written permission of the authors, or authorization through payment of the appropriate per-copy fee to the authors. Requests to the author for permission should be sent by email to: beth@defendandpublish.com or beth.hewett@gmail.com

ISBN: 978-0-9997623-2-5

Good Words Publishing, Forest Hill, MD
www.bethhewett.com

Contents

How To Use This Guide 1

Introduction 5

Chapter 1 - Targeting A Journal 9
    Identifying What To Write About 10
    Consider What Angle You Would Like To Take 12
    Finding The Right Journal/S For Your Article 14
        Figure 1: Finding The Right Journal For Your Article 18
    Evaluating Whether The Journal Is Right For Your Publication 18
        Figure 2: Is The Journal Right For Your Publication? 21
    Print Versus Online 21
    Submission Guidelines 23
    Self-Plagiarism: The Conundrum Of Reusing Your Own Words And Data 26
    Pre-Submission Communication: Priming The Pump 28
        Summary 1 - Targeting A Journal 30

Chapter 2 - Structuring The Article 33
    Some Article Types 34
    Some Parts Of An Article 35
        Abstract 36
        Introduction 37
        Literature Review 38
        Research Method 41
        Results 43
        Conclusion 45
        Figure 3 - Some Parts Of An Academic Article 46

References 45

Single And Coauthoring: The Good, Bad, And Ugly 47

    Single Authoring 48

    Coauthoring 50

    Purpose 53

Article Structure 55

    Example 1 - Ieee Author Information 57

Knowing Your Audience And Occasion 56

    Audience 58

    Occasion 59

Word Count And Article Length 60

    Summary 2 - Structuring The Article 63

Chapter 3 - Revising & Editing 65

Drafting And Revising An Article 65

The Layers Of Revision And Editing 67

    Revision 67

    Editing 68

        Figure 4 - Layers Of Revising, Editing & Proofreading 70

        Abstract Moving Through The Revision Process 71

        Example 2 - Abstract Moving Through Revision Process 71

    Proofreading 72

        Summary 3 - Revising & Editing 75

Chapter 4 - Submission & Review Process 77

Submitting Your Article 77

    Example 3 - Elsevier Submission Check List For Authors (Partial) 78

Writing A First Letter/Email Of Submission 80

V

  What Comes After Submission? 81
    Editor And/Or Reviewer Comments 82
      Figure 5 - Editor And/Or Reviewer Comments 86
  Reading And Interpreting Editor And Reviewer Comments 87
    Example 4 - Author's Reaction To Reviewers' Comments [Original] 88
    Addressing Editor And Reviewer Comments 89
    Example 5 - Author's Reaction To Reviewers' Comments [Revised] 89
  Revising The Article 90
  Writing A Second Email/Letter Of Submission 91
    Summary 4 - Submission & Review Process 91

Chapter 5 - What's Next 93
  You Were Published! What's Next? 93
  Proofs And Galleys 93
  Showing Appreciation 94
  Digital Access Publications Options 94
  Sharing Your Good News 95
  You Didn't Get Published. What's Next? 95
    When Should You Move On To Another Journal? 96
    From Rejection To (Re)Submission 97
  Last Words 98
    Summary 5 - What's Next 99

Acknowledgements 101

About the Authors 103
  Beth L. Hewett, Ph.D. 103
  Robbin Z. Warner, Ph.D. 104

How to Use This Guide

This guide addresses the needs of academic writers from the brand spanking new writer to the novice writer to even the writer with one or two published articles. The new and novice writer may want to read this guide from cover to cover whereas the more experienced writer will find certain sections more helpful and others too elementary. Use this guide as it makes sense to you.

Also, read this guide with attention to how your own discipline's journals and collected edition books work. If you're an experienced writer, you may know some ways that your field's written genres differ or are similar. If you're a novice scholarly writer, take what you learn here and then check in with a mentor or writing coach regarding questions for your discipline's conventions.

We wrote this guide for writers who want or need to publish non-book projects in academe. This audience includes new scholars who need to publish in order to be considered for full-time jobs, as well as academics who need to publish for tenure and promotion purposes. This guide will help international scholars understand some of the customs for publishing in American settings. We also consider the needs and desires of scholars who may be publishing for other reasons such as the simple desire—or even a passion—to convey their ideas about past research, theoretical concerns, and educational practices. Please note that book projects (i.e., monographs, coauthored books, and edited collections) require some different approaches.

Although there are no hard and fast rules for publishing a scholarly article, book chapter, or other (non-book) manuscript, it's possible to learn tips, tricks, and tactics from published authors and journal editors. This guidebook offers practical strategies for getting published, many of which pertain across disciplinary fields. While no one strategy applies to all disciplines, most can be adapted to one's field.

We offer this guidebook as a beginning point for writing and finding the right publishing venue for your project. Although we don't address in depth all the writing aspects of preparing the project (e.g., brainstorming, prewriting, drafting) for publication, we do consider the basic parts and tasks of writing to publish. Remember that writing coaches and other mentors, as well as other books, also can assist with the writing prior to attempting to publish. Ultimately, you may not know what help you need until you've attempted your first article manuscript.

It's okay to be a new or novice writer. Every publishing scholar started at some time with a first article draft. What's not okay is to submit an article draft to an editor that isn't ready for review. In other words, it's not a good idea to look like a novice or give the impression of not being ready to publish. We wrote this guide to help you through the publishing process, so you not only understand the steps involved but know how to navigate each one.

All scholarly writers should take these steps:

1. Know and read the key journals in your discipline. Be aware of the ongoing conversation about particular topics and theories. Make an educated decision about which conversations you're ready to join before diving in.

2. Read, read, read. Read whatever you can in your discipline before you begin writing and read even more while you're writing. It's your responsibility to know your disciplinary field's interests, core philosophies, theoretical biases, and preferred genre styles.

3. Never try to publish in a journal that you haven't read. In fact, given that your article is supposed to be a part of an ongoing conversation in the field, plan to include in your draft at least one or more articles as source support from the intended journal.

4. Always check the author guidelines, as we discuss in this guidebook. Pay attention to what you're asked to do. Editors read your thoughtfulness in this area as credibility and evidence of your ability to research carefully.

5. Ask the editor if you have questions or concerns about whether your idea is a good fit for the journal or book collection. Editors

are always looking for top-notch material, and they can direct you to other venues if theirs isn't appropriate. They also can instruct you in shaping your piece in a direction that works for them.

Features of the Guide:

We have developed Publishing an Academic Article: Tips, Tricks, and Tactics with a series of features designed to help you find the information you need quickly.

- A clear breakdown of the steps in the writing and revising processes.

- Case studies of writer problems and solutions.

- Examples from journal submissions guidelines.

- Figures that highlight specific aspects of writing for publication

- Textbox callouts:

    Tips & Tricks – Handy tools and strategies for getting your writing published.

    Advice from a Published Author – First-hand accounts from published authors.

    An Editor's Note – Journal editors discuss what they wish writers knew before submitting an article.

- Summary graphic of each chapter, useful as teaching and learning handouts.

Introduction

Max is an American who lives in Japan. He's working on his PhD at a Japanese university where the dissertation consists of the traditional five chapters (i.e., problem statement and background, literature review, methods, data results, and synthesis). However, he's not allowed to defend the dissertation until he has published two articles from his research. It's a stiff requirement, but it's not unlike other non-traditional dissertations that require students to write and submit (and/or publish) two articles as part of their capstone project.

Andrea is an assistant professor seeking tenure in a social sciences discipline at an American university. She has conducted several studies and is in the process of writing them up for publication. Although her tenure process doesn't require a book, it does require a minimum of three well-placed articles in known journals. She's never considered herself a good writer, and she's worried that she won't be able to meet the university's tenure requirements.

Max and Andrea share the same problems as new scholars. What do they need to know in order to publish well-written articles? How can they find the right journals for their ideas? In a market of tight competition, how can they get published? What do published writers know that they don't know?

Most likely, nobody is going to teach them or you how to write a publishable article. In fact, your own dissertation advisor or department chair or any other mentor may know what's involved from personal experience, but they may not be able to articulate that knowledge (however, a good writing coach such as those at Defend & Publish certainly can help you).

Nonetheless, writing a publishable article is a teachable/learnable process. It's a skill with identifiable techniques and methods. In fact, much like a dissertation, a scholarly article (or even an edited book chapter) tends to have recipe-like features that help authors earn a publication.

Tips & Tricks

Although we reference journals as the main publishing venue in this guide, our tips also apply to chapters of edited book collections. In edited books, however, editors may monitor author style and content more closely or differently to achieve greater consistency across the book.

Targeting a Journal

So, you need to have some publications or, at a minimum, potentially publishable manuscripts to achieve your academic goals. There are various ways to go about this process.

One way is simply to write an article—perhaps restructuring a seminar paper, culling research from your dissertation, or formulating research on an entirely new topic. Then, choose a journal and send out the article. Since journal editors typically state in their submission requirements that multiple submissions aren't allowed, you're on the honor system to send the piece only to one journal at a time. This process has the advantage of being fairly straightforward: just open a page of journal titles and throw a dart to choose one! Or pick the top journal in your discipline and hope for the best.

We recommend a third way to go about getting published: be strategic. Think of it as publication matchmaking—the right article for the right journal at the right time. All three have to align for it to be the right match.

In this strategic process, you follow a series of steps to achieve your goal:

1. Identify the scholarly or intellectual work you have produced that you want to communicate.

2. Consider what angle you want to take.

3. Evaluate possible journals to approach.

ADVICE FROM A PUBLISHED WRITER

If you're seeking promotion and/or tenure, check the status of journals with your promotion and tenure committee. I have learned that if the top journal in your field doesn't want your piece, you need to know where to go next and what counts in your department and institution—and you need to be able to make an argument for such choices. This step is particularly important in multi-discipline departments where promotion and tenure committee members may not know that a certain journal is the top one in your field, even though it looks dodgy to them. This problem happened to a colleague who was in a newly blended department of library and computer sciences. He published several articles with journals well-regarded in his field, but the new department chair didn't think they were credible given his own disciplinary orientation. That impression lingered throughout the entire promotion and tenure process; ultimately, he was denied tenure.

Identifying What to Write About

The first step is to identify the scholarly or intellectual work you have produced that you want to communicate. Identifying what to write about is a major part of getting published. People who publish a lot don't do so just because people like them or because they have a magic touch. They publish because they do interesting and important research, speak to contemporary topics—whether arguing for or against them—and actually help to create the next hot topic. They publish because they have something to say that others need to know.

You should write about something you've researched and want to communicate. Papers that make it to publication typically reveal the results or products of one's intellectual activity. Although many scholars have an impetus to publish because of their job search or promotion and tenure requirements, others want to publish to connect with the ongoing conversation in their field and to share study results and new approaches. Ask yourself:

- What thread of your work do you want to focus on?

- What do you want the field to be talking about?

- What should they be talking about?
- How can you contribute to that goal?

We certainly appreciate the need to publish for employment purposes, but that requirement wasn't developed as a mere hurdle to overcome and then to ignore after promotion and tenure. Publishing isn't something extraneous to the work that's happening in our various disciplines or teaching; publishing is what's happening in our disciplines or teaching. Publishing isn't a separate, scary thing that only the best, most confident, and smartest people can do. Publishing is our job as academics. Moreover, writing up an intellectual product just because you need a publication for your CV—from purely a drudge work perspective—leads to less-than-stellar writing and uninteresting papers that often fail to get published.

ADVICE FROM A PUBLISHED WRITER

My motivation for my first article was wanting to tell people about the gap I saw in our discipline. I wanted to talk to more than the six people who came to my conference presentation or my best friend who was sick of hearing me talk about it. I wanted to publish because I had a point (what I saw as an important point) that I wanted to add to the intellectual conversation on the topic.

To get published, you need to have something interesting to say. To publish frequently, you need something of potential *foundational value*, something that strongly influences later developments and that others will respond to and replicate, support and continue, or even object to in meaningful ways. In scholarly publishing, it isn't a bad thing to be polemic in approach. Other scholars' opinions are needed to help the discipline make strides and refine ideas. In fact, one of your goals should be to publish ideas that others will cite, agree with, extend, or refute.

Of course, it's important to know what approach certain journals take and whether they would even be amenable to your specific approach—or whether your piece would find external reviewing readers who are open-minded. If you know that you're proposing something controversial, then check with the editors to see whether it's something they would consider before you send it in and go through the process.

That said, research usually isn't giant leaps—it's incremental work taken one small step at a time. One piece builds on another. It's one puzzle piece of a much larger puzzle. The work doesn't have to be "new" or even on a grand scale to make a different point or add to disciplinary thinking. Consider it this way: from the outside we may see seismic shifts, but if you look at a discipline or author's body of work, you can see them working out these ideas in small chunks.

ADVICE FROM A PUBLISHED WRITER

I think novice writers struggle with knowing how to write for a broader audience as opposed to writing for a mentor or committee. This audience focus means knowing how to read and join the conversation by making small steps, not having to feel like you have the latest and most brilliant idea. Small changes and modest articles can be important and publishable.

Consider What Angle You Would Like to Take

Any article idea needs not only a thesis—or an argument—which should emerge from your completed research, but also an angle from which you want to address that thesis. Sometimes that research is empirical in nature, and other times it's more theoretical and based in a new reading of the existing literature. Either way, your work involves framing a question and defining a research focus; the article itself fulfills that purpose.

Think about these questions:

- Do you want to write something informative (i.e., expository) or polemical (i.e., argumentative)?
- Do you want to report on your study's data results?

- Do you want to elicit change or confirm the status quo?
- Do you want to teach your colleagues educational strategies that work in particular settings?
- Do you want to fill a gap in the research literature with a study that you've conducted?
- Do you want to argue for a new perspective or framework on an existing topic or question?

Any of these goals are good reasons for writing a paper on the topic of your choice.

This guide walks you through the entire publication process once you've decided on a topic: journal selection, writing the piece, revising it, sending it to various editors and arguing for it through submission letters, and the like. Your topic may shift and change throughout the writing and submission processes, and it may further shift as you revise from reviewers' feedback. That's okay. Such changes are refinements of your thinking and writing, and these are natural and

TIPS & TRICKS

You're not responsible for completing the entire 5000-piece puzzle of a research, educational, or intellectual problem—only one piece of it.

AN EDITOR'S NOTE

Many new PhDs don't immediately understand the importance of being edited. They might get upset or even angry when an editor makes suggestions of substantive revisions. Avoid the temptation to think of your writing as inviolate and perfect. It's a hard lesson to learn, but it's an important one. The well published writers will be the first to tell you to listen to your editor.

necessary parts of the process. Although it may feel like you're being told to change your perspective or that you've done something wrong in your initial paper, these changes suggest that people are interested in what you want to say and are helping you to refine your approach. Therefore, take such advice as a positive sign. Everyone needs an editor!

Finding the Right Journal/s for Your Article

The process of finding the right journals for your article is a bit like the process of finding the right topic. You likely won't be published if you don't know what people are talking about in the field, and that conversation is found in the journals and collected-article books that exist or are just being published while you're doing your research or scholarly activity, thinking, and writing. The current conversation is one with which you need to be familiar; more importantly, it's what you want to join. However, because publishing venues may be scarce and are especially important to new scholars who need to demonstrate their research chops, joining the conversation means extending it or contributing to it in a significant (but likely a small) way—or finding a new way to view or shake up a current idea that is challenging the field. That's why dissertations often contain excellent material for at least one publication of relevance and interest to the discipline.

How do you locate the right journal for your article? There's no one right way. Following are some basic strategies, which are summarized in Figure 1.

AN EDITOR'S NOTE

> When I was a novice writer, I wish I had known how to read academic journals purposefully in order to grasp their style and conventions and then how to build that understanding into a proposal or draft. All of my early journal publications emerged out of conference presentations and were pretty happenstance. I did get two articles published as a graduate student, mostly because I had some (very raw) talent with writing. At the time, I lacked a coherent writing process. I assumed one could only write when inspired, which I rarely was. I lacked discipline and structure and was resistant to following directions and guidance.

Journals You Read: Start by looking at the publications you're already reading. These could be publications in your field or in other fields. Because you're already reading them, you know the intended audience because you are that audience. As you read through these journals, think about the writing styles and approaches they accept. Which one/s tend to match your potential topic, angle, writing style, or other interests?

Journals Already Publishing Articles on Your Topic: The next place to look is the reference lists of the articles and books you're reading related to your article's topic. Annotated bibliographies and other texts' reference lists will lead to more articles, which in turn lead to more reference lists to peruse. Finally, dissertations are a great resource because the reference lists tend to be comprehensive.

AN EDITOR'S NOTE

Novice writers need to do research on journals. It's a mistake to submit to a journal you haven't read; while it's possible to get published under those circumstances, it's not the optimal. The lack of knowledge typically shows in submissions and is often a turnoff for regular reviewers/editorial board members. Scholarly publishing is about joining a conversation on issues and concerns related to a field.

Therefore, think and act the way good authors do:

- Research the journal and its typical topics, canonical authors, and standard citation practices.

- Revise your work sufficiently so that the piece can stand alone as a theoretical or data-driven research article. Many new scholars base their publication submissions on their dissertation work, for example, and make the mistake of referring to "chapters" that no longer exist.

- Move beyond the standard literature review to have a point of significance about a topic. While it's important to cite canonical work, it's vital to move beyond that gesturing to clarify how the author is adding to the conversation.

Think about your own discipline's preferences for dated materials. The humanities tend to value both current and past texts depending on their fundamental value to the field. Literary criticism and history are two among these. The social sciences certainly value current publications particularly as they may take foundational ideas and apply new thinking to them. Some of the sciences (e.g., biology, chemistry, engineering, and mathematics) advance so quickly that only the most recent pieces are useful. For example, *Cell*, a biology journal, has so many excellent submissions that move the field forward at a rapid pace that they publish every two weeks.

Graduate Course Material and Mentor's CVs: Authors need to have both depth and breadth when it comes to places to publish, and many of those who don't publish probably don't have that. Likely, many schools don't explicitly teach or address the useful skill of learning about where (and how) to publish. However, graduate course syllabi and texts do lead the wise student to helpful resources. It's also useful for students to look at their teachers' and mentors' CVs, as well as the published CVs of disciplinary leaders, to find different publication venues.

Calls for Papers/Project (CFPs): You can find CFPs at the back of some print journals, posted on popular disciplinary listservs, on journal websites, and even on Facebook groups (e.g., Medieval Studies Calls for Papers). Sometimes CFPs are targeted to particular topics, like special issues of a journal or an edited collection. Other times, they're more general and simply call for articles relative to the discipline. CFPs offer specific ideas for the issue through the explanations they provide and questions they pose for scholars to consider. They provide good information both for forming an article and for writing about it in a letter of submission.

Google It: Google has several resources for identifying scholarly journals. Even though a Google search isn't the most targeted approach, you never know what might pop up. As the Google option says, "Are you feeling lucky?" Start with a simple Google search. Then move onto Google Scholar, a Google service that only searches scholarly literature. Searching a topic on Google Scholar is a quick way to see your topic through the lens of an expanded disciplinary universe of scholarly research. Additionally, it offers the bonus feature of seeing how many times particular articles are cited by other scholars, which both indicates the importance of a topic and the benefit of certain articles to your own literature review.

Work with a Librarian: Work with your institution's librarians to research journals. Contemporary librarians are experts in online research, and they can teach you what you need to know about using the most recent search engines as well as help you form your online search strategy using the best keywords and strategies. Take advantage of this service. Research librarians appreciate it when you seek their assistance; that's an essential part of their job. This resource is something scholars advise students to do, but often forget to use themselves.

Expand Your Scope: We tend to look in the directories and in the online locations we know. Try expanding your research universe for journal possibilities. For example, check whether an international journal might be appropriate. Also, consider a new online-only journal that's just getting started and other multimodal and multidisciplinary journals. Be aware, though, that newer journals may not yet count toward tenure or promotion if they're online or haven't yet established their credibility. That said, some new journals have top-notch scholars developing and editing them. Look over their material and talk with a mentor about the journal's potential.

Ask Colleagues: Finally, network with colleagues—especially formal mentors—to discuss where you should try to publish. People love to give advice. Ask them how they got their own publications. You can post this query on Facebook or on listservs you follow. You can reach out to colleagues through email or when you see them at conferences and professional meetings. While not necessarily your personal friends, colleagues care about the disciplinary field and the quality of work that people like you produce.

Figure 1: Finding the Right Journal for Your Article

Evaluating Whether the Journal Is Right for Your Publication

Once you've identified a journal as a potential place to publish, it's time to evaluate whether the journal is right for your article. Such evaluation engages the following steps, which are summarized in Figure 2.

Author Guidelines: Start by reading the author guidelines. They usually identify the intended audience, and typically they're thorough about what potential authors need to consider. But you will need to do more than this initial effort. Sometimes the journal is going in a new direction and the editors are in the process of updating published guidelines. Or, if you're planning to submit an article draft to a

ADVICE FROM A PUBLISHED WRITER

If you're trying to strengthen your tenure or employment dossier, be familiar with the stated and unstated metrics that your department and college use. Be sure to follow those metrics. You need to know whether your academic department or institution requires a certain number of publications in high-profile journals and whether they will consider publications in less well-known journals as being "half" of one in a high-profile journal.

You also need to know whether web-based journals will be sufficiently well regarded for your publications. Despite a strong trend of blind reviews and high-quality publications in many web journals, some institutions, like mine, still don't respect online journals or hold them in as high a regard as traditional print-only journals or those whose beginnings were in a print-only era. If you choose web-based journals (and many are quite good), be prepared to argue for your choice. I've done it successfully as have several of my colleagues. I'm sure that soon we won't need to argue for the validity of web-based journals.

TIPS & TRICKS

If the editor's email isn't published, search for the editor online; check for the institutional email if there is one.

special issue or edited book collection, the author guidelines or other necessary information may not be as clear. You won't know this until you dig a little further. An email to the editor may clarify things for you. Additionally, you can email the editor with your idea (using just a few sentences) and ask whether your piece is something he or she would consider or be interested in. If you're uncertain, it's a good idea to ask questions; experienced scholars do this all the time.

Read Back Issues: Read through a year or two of the journal's back issues. Pay attention to what subject matter and types of articles have been published versus what the guidelines say will be published. As you do, identify topics, themes, perspectives, and genres of interest.

Writing Style: Check the journal's writing style. Is it jargon heavy and focusing on a specific audience, or does the writing style make topics accessible to a broad audience? Do authors write in the first person or is the prose more formally third person? You're making these observations to determine whether the journal's writing style is one in which you're comfortable working.

Is the Journal's Intended Audience Your Article's Right Audience? Consider the intended audience to determine whether and why they would want to read about your topic.

- Is your topic already part of the conversation in this field/journal?

- Are you a member of this community and want to apply your field's approach to this topic?

- Did you find this journal because they're doing a special issue on your topic?

- Do you want to introduce something new into an ongoing conversation? This approach is what more established scholars typically do, and you can do it too.

- How could you join the ongoing conversation in this community?

AN EDITOR'S NOTE

The number one mistake novice writers make is pitching proposals and articles that are not relevant to the mission of the journal. Read the directions, please! A close second is failing to be familiar with the conversations going on in the field and in a journal. Overstating the originality or impact of an article also is a big problem.

Is the Journal Right for Your Publication?

- Read the author guidelines
- Read through back issues
- Check the journal's writing style
- Is the journal's intended audience your article's right audience?

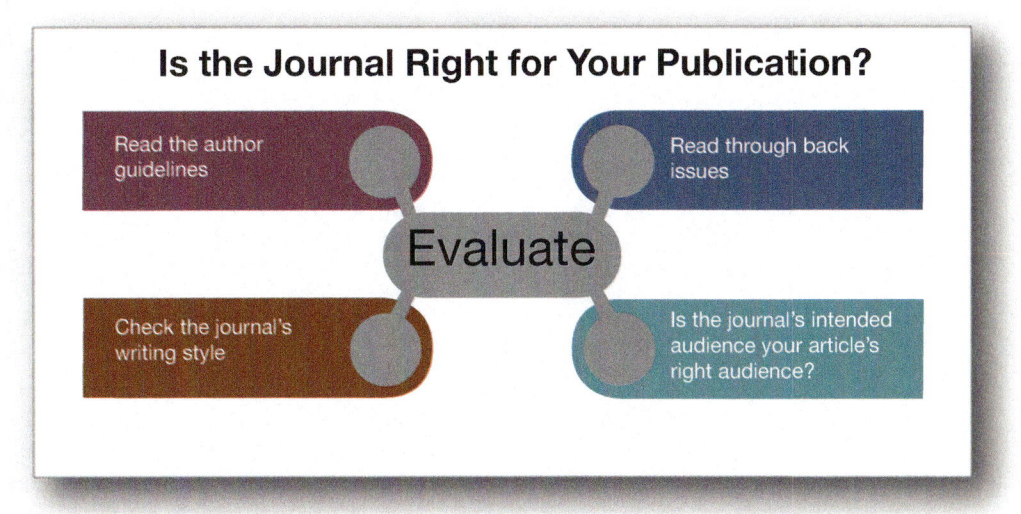

Evaluate

Figure 2: Is the Journal Right for Your Publication?

Print versus Online

Things are changing in the publishing world. Where print once ruled in terms of publication prestige, raw economics have leveled the parity playing field, removing the stigma of online publications for many academics and their mentors or administrators. A journal's quality doesn't automatically change just because it's published online—even though that's what many academics once thought. Anonymous, or blind, reviewed texts still are the gold standard regardless of delivery options. Currently, many new scholarly journals are deciding to publish solely online for cost reasons. Nearly all print-based publications now have online editions or portable document format (PDF) options for accessing issues, making delivering scholarship online an established and respected part of the academic landscape. Few publications can afford to ignore the power of being online and accessible to many more readers.

Frequently, hardcopy journals in the sciences and humanities also have online versions that embed links to expanded sections on technical method, technical calculations, tables of data, multimodal content, and outside resources. Some journals are both print-based and online, some are primarily print-based with some appendix-like online features, and others are fully online.

TIPS & TRICKS

Double-blind reviews are when reviewers don't know who authors are, and authors don't know who reviewers are. Single-blind reviews are when reviewers know who authors are, but authors don't know who reviewers are.

TIPS & TRICKS

When evaluating a recently launched journal—whether print-based or online—make sure it has appropriate credentials. For example, the journal should have an association with a scholarly society or more than a year of issues with well-written, theoretically sound articles.

It's also important to pay attention to membership requirements. Some journals require that you be a dues-paying member of their society before you can submit articles, some require membership before the actual publication, and others are open in that area. Know the rules for the journal and whether you financially can afford to submit to it.

Some fully online journals present their articles in a traditional appearance; in other words, except that the paper is delivered online, it has all the traditional paper-based features and can be printed as a whole in a PDF format. Other online journals present articles in nontraditional forms that encourage short paragraphs for better online readability, multimodal features, and hyperlinking to other pages (called nodes). This means that instead of presenting your argument only through alphabetic text and more common multimodal features such as charts, tables, and/or images, the journal takes advantage of the functionality of an online setting. These features include the ability to chunk the text by nodes and to hyperlink them, which enables and encourages readers to choose the organizational strategy for their reading. They also include other multimodal features such as audio, video, interactive comment/response sections, and other digital tools. If your topic would benefit from this type of format, then consider seeking out such a publication.

There are several benefits of publishing in online journals. One benefit is that they often can publish longer articles or are more flexible in word count because they aren't bound by the costs of print. Moreover, online journals sometimes have the flexibility to add articles to issues already in the pipeline for faster turn-around. Finally, online publications that are open access rather than tied to a subscription tend to reach a broader audience because they can be found through readily available search features.

That said, when preparing a webtext for an online journal, you must work with the editor to attend to issues of accessibility. For video and audio features, you must provide transcripts that sight-disabled readers can translate to large print or use with text-to-speech devices, which may be optical or electronic. Such transcripts also aid hearing disabled readers who cannot hear the audio portions of a video or the provided audio file. PDF files must be access enabled. For still images, there must be captions that have thick, rich descriptions to enable sight-disabled readers to know what the media is and why it's there. Although such accessibility concerns might seem off-putting at first, a few quick lessons from one's IT department or advice from a guide such as provided by the World Wide Web Consortium (W3C), the international body that establishes web standards, will reveal how simple this process can be. By the way, if the online journal you're submitting to doesn't discuss access with you automatically, raise the subject yourself. If they don't take access seriously, we think you should avoid publishing with them. The Americans with Disabilities Act rightly states that access to all people is a critical, basic right.

Submission Guidelines

The first step after choosing a target publication is to review the publication's submission guidelines. They might be called "Submission Guidelines," "Author Guidelines," "Notes to Authors," or any number of titles. All publications have them and the editors and reviewers will expect you to know the publication's requirements. Both the editors and reviewers will notice whether you follow the guidelines.

Most journals also will indicate both their disciplinary field's focus as well as possible points of topical focus. For example, the American

Psychologist is the official journal of the American Psychological Association, which publishes timely high-impact papers of broad interest whereas the Scholarship of Teaching and Learning in Psychology has a much narrower focus. Authors should pay attention to those points of focus as well as the other specs offered under the Submission Guidelines. Reading these can be especially helpful when trying to publish an article in a niche journal, in a journal crossing disciplinary boundaries, or in a journal targeted to a field other than your own but developing a special issue that intersects with your area of expertise.

Although guidelines can vary in terms of focus and thoroughness, expect to find the following:

- **Citation style:** A publication will identify the style guide and the edition it follows for formatting in-text citations, footnotes, endnotes, and references. For example, a journal in the humanities might use the Modern Languages Association (MLA) Handbook or The Chicago Manual of Style while a journal in the social sciences will use the American Psychological Association (APA) Handbook. Medical doctors—as well as certain other scientific fields—will use the American Medical Association (AMA) style. Many other discipline-specific styles exist. In fact, some journals detail a hybrid style only they use. Reviewers will know the style of the journal and expect it to be followed. If the author fails to follow the style, the reviewer might assume that if the author is sloppy with citations, perhaps the research also is sloppy. Be aware that style manual editions can change without much notice. New editions can feature significantly new citation and formatting style rules, so keep up with your discipline's (or that specific journal's) style requirements.
- **Word count:** A publication will list the word count and/or article length allowable for each type of article it publishes. Don't exceed word count without good reason.
- **Submission process:** Most publications now use an online submission process where an article is either submitted through email or an online submission form. All steps in the submission process need to be followed. Failing to follow the

process completely could result in the article being rejected.

- **One journal at a time:** Most journals explicitly state that you may submit only to one journal at a time. Sometimes you must attest in writing that you agree to that stipulation. Don't risk your integrity with an end run around this requirement. Making sure that your article is formatting in the house style is one way of assuring the editor and reviewers that you're following that stipulation to the letter.

- **Review process:** One of the cornerstones of an academic journal is the peer review process. The publication will explain its process for reviewing article submissions. Some publications, but not all, give a time estimate for the review process, which means you don't have to ask the editor in advance. If there's no review process (which happens with some journals), then think carefully about whether you want to publish there. Most jobs search or tenure committees will discount non-peer-reviewed pieces.

AN EDITOR'S NOTE

Read the guidelines. Follow the guidelines. They're requirements, not suggestions.

AN EDITOR'S NOTE

It's critical to check your quotes and references for correctness. Don't expect the editors to do the work of formatting citations for you. Journal editors lament that manuscripts rarely have accurate references pages or quotations.

Self-Plagiarism: The Conundrum of Reusing Your Own Words and Data

> *Karl had completed everything required for his PhD when he was informed he had a problem that might prevent him from graduating. In his program, he first had to publish two articles on his research. Only then was he allowed to complete and defend his dissertation. After he sent his dissertation draft to his committee chair, he received comments that shocked him. He was being accused of self-plagiarism because he had reused phrases, sentences, paragraphs, and figures verbatim from his published articles. Karl thought: The material in those articles was from my own dissertation research, so why can't I use it in the dissertation itself? How can I plagiarize myself anyway? I'm not stealing someone else's ideas. This is my research and my own words!*

Plagiarism occurs when writers present someone else's words and ideas as their own—purposefully or not—without proper attribution and citation. The lack of attribution and citation signals to readers that the material is original to the writer; yet, in cases of plagiarism, this signal is false. Scholars are supposed to know better, and undergraduate students routinely learn quotation, paraphrase, and citation requirements for using other's material. Simply, plagiarism is theft of others' ideas and content, and it isn't acceptable in academic (or other) writing.

If plagiarism has to do with using other people's material inappropriately, how can using, or reusing, your own published content in another essay, article, or monograph like a dissertation be a form of stealing?

The answer is that self-plagiarism isn't really about theft although the situation can seem to be just that. Instead, there's a nuanced quality to this problem that outright plagiarism doesn't have. Self-plagiarism is when you present previously published content (i.e., text, data, figures, tables, or images) as if it is new material without letting the reader or the publication know that the material is being reused. In other words, self-plagiarism ultimately is about misleading the reader and/or the new publication regarding the origin and previous uses of the content.

Self-plagiarism comes in many forms. For example, one might publish the same article in more than one publication venue without letting readers or the publication venues know this has occurred. Such republication is considered reprehensible and can end one's career. In other instances, self-plagiarism consists of slicing, dicing, and/or reanalyzing data without letting the reader know that the data are from a larger study and have been aggregated, disaggregated, or segmented for this article. Sometimes, self-plagiarism comes in the form of recycling sections of text, like a literature review or methodology section. Still other times, it is using the same material, but in different venues, such as from conference to conference, conference to journal or book, or, as in Karl's case, from journal article to dissertation.

The nuance is that the writer both owns the original ideas and content and doesn't own them simultaneously. This problem is because, once published, the material typically comes under the copyright of the publisher—a journal, for example—and the ownership is transferred to the publication.

In many cases, self-plagiarism can be easily avoided by three actions:

First, contact the publisher of the originally published article, book, or dissertation. Ask for permission to reprint verbatim parts of the text and/or images or to reuse the material in any other manner. Typically, such permission is granted and the approved method for such citation is provided, to include internal citation and bibliographic standards as well as any other necessary acknowledgements. Follow these standards precisely.

Second, paraphrase whatever material you can, saving direct quotation for content you cannot otherwise rephrase because it already has been phrased best for your current uses. Avoid directly citing full paragraphs and multiple paragraphs wherever possible. Frankly, it's likely you can state the ideas better for the new context because the point of view shifts at least slightly with each publication.

Third, acknowledge where the material was previously used or published by citing yourself as the source. Thorough and regular self-citation inspires confidence in readers that whatever has not been cited as your own or someone else's previously published material is, in fact, original content to this particular piece.

Finally, note that when writing articles or books from dissertations, it's best to acknowledge that the content comes from the dissertation (which is the opposite situation that Karl had in this section's opening scenario). In many cases, the dissertation is considered to be published when it's made available by the graduate school to a wider audience. Often, such acknowledgement can be a simple statement in the beginning of the text or in a footnote. When in doubt, ask your publisher about the preferred style.

Pre-submission Communication: Priming the Pump

Once you've decided on a journal, consider communicating with the editor or a member of the editorial board. If the journal is in your field, you might already know one of these people. Association meetings and conferences often have sessions where journal editors are available to speak to potential authors and provide their business cards. Make use of these opportunities. Editors want to meet you; they're hoping your proposed article might be the best they've ever published. Personal connections and networking are an important part of the publication process.

Benefits of Communicating with Editor: Nora's Story

Nora found out about the publication of a special issue of a journal on her topic of research just four weeks before the submission deadline. Although she had an article topic in mind, the piece was not going to be ready in time. Nora emailed the editor, presenting her paper topic and asking for an extension. Not only did the editor give Nora a three-week extension, but the email started a conversation on her topic with the editor that ultimately resulted in the article being accepted in the special issue.

Benefits of Communicating with Editor: Kenji's Story

After Kenji's article was rejected by a journal that he had thought was a natural fit, he had to search for a new publication. He asked around and discovered a journal that appeared perfect for the manuscript's focus. Kenji then emailed the editor to inquire whether the journal would be interested in an article on his topic. The editor was interested, offered some advice for what he especially would be looking for, and encouraged Joe to submit soon. After two rounds of reviewer's feedback and comprehensive edits, not only was his article accepted, but it was inserted into the issue coming out that month, making it a wonderfully short (and rare) turnaround time.

Of course, neither of these stories is an example of how papers usually get published in science. If a writer has a new result that is relevant in understanding or testing a model or theory, the paper typically gets published if it's well-written (or able to be revised appropriately) and technically correct. If there are challenges, they're typically found in:

- Demonstrating that the result is new: For example, previous measurements were with chemical X (or animal A) and this new result is with chemical Y (or animal B). How is the result applicable?

- The current paradigm expects chemical X (animal A) to behave like chemicals R, S, T, and U (animals J, K, and L) but you found that it doesn't. How can you explain that result?

In both of these cases, the speed with which scientific articles are reviewed and published may make it best simply to submit the paper and ask questions after the reviews come in.

These points aside, good authors communicate well. A few well-written, brief emails can really help build a connection with an editor and often result in a better article as well as a smoother process. When authors drop off the radar for weeks at a time, editors don't assume that no news is good news. They assume that nothing is happening in the writing or rewriting. So, stay in touch and let your editor (and coauthors) know how the work is progressing (or not).

ADVICE FROM A PUBLISHED WRITER

I want to stress the importance of having contact with editors. At a recent conference, I made it a point to go to their personal sessions and to attend a panel that included several publication venues and editors even though I had to decline a ride to the airport with my boss and had to sprint to my flight. It was well worth it. I was able to have good one-on-one conversations with two editors who helped me frame my ideas and are interested in seeing my future work.

SUMMARY - Targeting a Journal

The 5 steps involved in targeting a journal for publication

Step 1	Communicate with the journal's editor before submitting your manuscript
Step 2	Research journals that could be right for your manuscript
Step 3	Determine whether a journal is right for your topic
Step 4	Spend time reviewing a journal's submission guidelines
Step 5	Communicate with the journal's editor before submitting your manuscript

Summary 1 - Targeting a Journal

2

Structuring the Article

Articles take different forms, or genres, depending on your disciplinary field, topic, goal, the type of research in which you engaged, and the journal you're targeting. For example, you might be writing up a scientific lab result, a theory-building article, applied research paper, literary analysis, literature review, exposition of teaching strategies with a teaching case, ethnographic research, or a case study. The necessary first step in structuring your article is determining the type of article you want to write.

Determining article type might be quite simple. Some people always write literary analyses. Period. That's what their field expects, and that's what they publish. Interestingly, while most scientists wouldn't think of writing anything other than scientific results, recently many humanists have begun to switch between arguing in more traditional genres and reporting the results of empirical studies. The field of rhetoric and composition is one such discipline. Scholars who wouldn't have ventured into ethnography, case study, teaching cases, and the like are now experimenting with different genres. That means they'll offer new perspectives in important areas. It also means they'll make some mistakes as they learn these genres. Scientists, too, might benefit from moving writing for new genres to publish in different or multidisciplinary journals.

The purpose of this chapter is not to provide an exhaustive list of article types or even of article structures. Return to your disciplinary journals, mentors, and graduate school methods courses for that list. We do, however, provide a taste of the variety of writing styles you might try within the bounds of your field's preferences and disciplinary requirements relative to job acquisition, promotion, and tenure. It's important to remember that writing an article is your part in an ongoing conversation with your colleagues.

ADVICE FROM A PUBLISHED WRITER

I think a great resource for figuring out what the purpose of your article is and how you can structure that (especially for the literature review—which builds the frame for your problem/issue/study/whatever) is Graff and Birkenstein's They Say / I Say: The Moves that Matter in Academic Writing (3rd ed., W.W. Norton. 2015). It's a great book for both reminding people that this work is a conversation, although on paper, and for thinking about meta-genres for articles.

Some Article Types

- **Scientific result:** A scientific result reports or communicates the findings of an experiment, calculation, or new analysis, usually within the context of how the findings test or confirm a theory or model.

- **Theory-building:** This genre extends or modifies existing theory so as to better describe (understand) existing data or data that recently have been measured and added to the world's data set. These types of papers typically use empirical data derived from and analyzed through quantitative, qualitative, or mixed methods.

- **Applied research:** Generally, applied research seeks to demonstrate how findings apply to such practices as teaching, counseling, engineering, psychology, and the like. Applied research papers in the sciences employ a technique or result from fundamental research to use it with a more real purpose (e.g., using nuclear magnetic resonance to scan a person's body and make images of the internal structures [NMR → MRI] or using quantum mechanical light amplification [lasers] to sculpt corneas).

- **Literary analysis:** This genre applies analytical procedures—typically ones that are well known and often used in the particular discipline—to historical and contemporary fiction and nonfiction. It can have a theoretical or contextual approach.

- **Literature review:** Also used as a part of a study's write up (discussed below), a literature review can be written as a stand-alone piece to analyze a theoretical or practical problem or to develop and suggest new theory or practices from past research. Scientific journals often invite specific people to write review articles based on the expertise of the people. These articles aren't part of a study's write up but rather a comprehensive and synergistic report. Annotated bibliographies might be considered within this genre.

- **Exposition of teaching strategies:** More of a practical article, the exposition of teaching strategies (particularly when contextualized by theory) explains how and/or why certain teaching approaches may work. These might include a teaching case or an application of other research. Typically, they have the goal of promoting one approach over others.

By the way, a book review may not be considered an article per se. A book review describes the genre of the book; summarizes its important points; offers a critical opinion of its value supported by examples from it and, possibly, past theories; compares it to others in its genre; and provides an informed opinion of its possible benefits for readers. The technology review uses much the same format to introduce and critically appraise new technologies for the intended audience.

Some Parts of an Article

Once you've determined the type of article you want to write, you're ready to focus on structuring it. Good authors tend to have a process and a routine, which is something a writing coach can help you develop. Journal articles are somewhat formulaic. There are forms and conventions that must be followed; doing so helps both writer and reader. There are different, identifiable parts to an article depending on the genre you've selected. These parts form a recipe-like approach, such that each author's unique content can be understood more readily by readers who anticipate receiving certain information in a rather standard arrangement, as explicated below and summarized in Figure 3.

AN EDITOR'S NOTE

Book and technology reviews typically aren't considered articles. It's an important distinction because a lot of newer faculty will put them under publications in their CVs and promotion portfolios as though they are articles, which can work against them in job searches and tenure evaluation. They should be on a CV but clearly marked as reviews.

Also, a lot of journals won't accept unsolicited book or technology reviews. Graduate students often aren't encouraged (or allowed) to write them because they don't have enough expertise in the field to critically evaluate the text or software/hardware. But it's important to note that these reviews—book reviews particularly—should include constructive criticism, not just criticism for the sake of it. Nastiness is too often a feature of book reviews because people act out personal vendettas in them, which is another reason graduate students don't usually do them. Such an error in tone or language can kill their career. It's important to stay objective and fair.

Let's review some of the parts of an article. Because doing so comprehensively is outside the scope of a brief guide to scholarly publishing, the discussion below often applies to the social sciences and the so-called hard sciences although humanities writers also are addressed. Writers from all disciplines can glean some connections among these parts and the article genres they typically write.

The parts of articles addressed in this chapter include an abstract, introduction, review of the literature, research methods, data results and analysis/discussion, conclusion, and references. Within those parts are subsections that help readers understand the major argument, or claim, of the piece.

Abstract

The abstract is a short paragraph of about 100 to 250 words as requested by the publication. It describes the problem the article addresses, summarizes research question/s or hypotheses, outlines the method used, indicates key results, and states the major findings. You can draft it easily by taking topic sentences from the paper and then revising those sentences by stressing key focal points and providing necessary transition phrases (these can be found in a style guide or handbook as well as on the Internet). Abstracts are best written after the article is complete.

Introduction

Sometimes the introductory section has no name. Other times, it's called the "Problem" or "Background of the Problem." Still other times, it's called by a contextually appropriate title that begins the story of the paper itself.

Indeed, the introduction narrates the story of the problem under consideration. It's key to readers understanding quickly why you've done the research or why you're writing the paper. The introduction responds to the following questions.

- What is the problem that the research is exploring?

- Why is it a problem? This part might be called the "background" in some journals.

- What have people tried to do about the problem? This also might be termed "background," but in scientific research reports, it might comprise a brief literature review.

- What are your research questions and/or hypotheses? How did you come to those questions or hypotheses?

- What is the purpose of your study?

- What is your claim, argument, or thesis and how did you arrive at that if not previously explained?

- Preview what you learned from the study. You cannot write this part, which comprises only a few sentences, until you actually know what you learned. Sometimes, this part is written last after you've concluded the article by summing up what you've learned.

It certainly would seem that anyone trying to publish would know this information about an introduction. Nonetheless, sometimes what one thinks is the easiest or most obvious gets overlooked. A good introduction all too often falls into this category.

TIPS & TRICKS

Publication style sheets are not all alike, as we've pointed out in Chapter 1. For example, although sections to academic articles typically have headings and subheadings to help guide readers through the organization of the material, sometimes (often with APA style) the introduction isn't labeled with a header. In those cases, headers begin after the introduction to identify subsequent sections and subsections.

Literature Review

What is called a "literature review" in the many of the social sciences and hard sciences is called a "historiography" in history. Be aware that your discipline may have another name for it. Whatever it's called, the review of the literature troubles many new academic writers. Perhaps they become stuck in bad memories of a 40-page literature review from their Master's thesis or PhD dissertation and now believe that all literature reviews have to be equally comprehensive.

Reading the journals in which you wish to publish will show that's not a good analogy. The literature review for an academic article is far shorter and has a different purpose. If it's labeled as a "literature review" at all, it tends to comprise about three to eight substantial paragraphs. When the entire journal article is a literature review, the discussion of various scholarly sources naturally will be much deeper, more detailed, and therefore lengthier. Nonetheless, such an article also needs an introduction and some of the other parts as described below.

Often, a review of pertinent literature is worked into the article's introduction. Its job is to help make connections with the original parts of your own work. One of the most strategic and challenging moves for a new academic writer is to push this discussion beyond the standard literature review to explicitly state a point of significance about a topic. The literature review helps you to explain the problem as it has been defined and addressed by others. It helps you to connect your work with what has come before. It also helps you to synthesize what scholars have done and said about this issue such that you can begin to illuminate your own paper's main (and new) points. While it's important to cite canonical work, it's more important to move beyond that gesturing to clarify how you as the author are adding to the conversation.

To this end, the literature review is a powerful tool for writers; planning and writing it allows you to begin to figure out where your work fits into the ongoing conversation. Your research into relevant published literature can help you to place where your own thinking and/or results fit with others' work, differ from previous thought, and point to new thinking. Work hard on this part of your writing in whatever way your discipline tends to structure it. Arguing outside of the published literature is like arguing in a vacuum.

ADVICE FROM A PUBLISHED WRITER

As writers, we have different styles and strategies that come from our own learning and thinking styles. For example, I have found that I must save all the articles from my literature review as digital copies. I also name the file to make it easy to find for article references. I used to save the article with an author's name and title, but later I realized that if there was a coauthor or even three, I needed these in the file name as well as the date. Now I use a reference organizer. There are lots available like Endnote, JabRef, and Mendeley. Google Scholar can also help organize your sources. That said, these tools have their limitations. You can't assume that everything is saved and/or formatted correctly. I know lots of people who don't use these tools precisely because they can introduce formatting errors or lose information added manually.

The literature review is the story of past research relative to the problem you outlined in the introduction. As such, it critically analyzes the research mentioned in this part of the article. When composing this section, consider the following:

- Acknowledge your point of view or reason for having selected the published literature you address. If you have a particular scholarly bias or agenda, acknowledge that.

- If your article is going to be long or especially complex, or if this strategy is typical in your discipline, provide a brief organizational guide to how the literature review is constructed. This may need to be written after the literature review proper is complete.

- Provide a brief summary of what you want the reader to take away from the review.

- Group the literature into themes (what the scholars studied), theories (how the scholars aligned themselves), and/or results (what the scholars learned from the studies). You also might group by methods: qualitative, quantitative, or mixed. Other organizational strategies may become obvious as you write.

- Within each theme or set of results, present material chronologically from earliest to most recent. Use subheadings if the literature review is lengthy. If the literature review is the article itself, use headings and subheadings to identify the themes.

- Pay attention to dates of the published research.

  - The social sciences and sciences prefer that research be timely and dated within the past five to ten years although older seminal research may need to be mentioned for context and to demonstrate historical awareness. Generally speaking, the more recent the source is, the better. These disciplines often—but don't always—use the APA citation style, which calls for past tense verbs when addressing previous studies (i.e., Johnson *stated, noted, acknowledged*, etc.).

  - The humanities—particularly history and literary criticism—tend to acknowledge the value of older research as it applies to the topic under discussion. Such a literature review might be a mix of older, foundational, and primary research with more recent research. These disciplines often use the MLA or Chicago citation styles, which call for present tense verbs when addressing previous studies (i.e., Johnson *states, notes, acknowledges*, etc.).

- Identify the author/s, date of the review, and—only if necessary—the full title of the published literature. Briefly summarize the research question or theme, how it was studied, and what the results were.

- Critically analyze the reviewed literature using such idea development and organizational strategies as definition, comparison, and cause and effect analysis.

- Finally, synthesize what the published literature reveals about the theme or results, how it advances knowledge, and/or what methodological strengths or weaknesses occur. Use the research and scholarship you've studied to clearly identify the "gap" of the literature that indicates a need for your study.

Advice from a Published Writer

I'm somewhat new at this publishing game, so I've found myself struggling with how to make notes for my lit review and organize it. Some people can do that right from the printed or online source article to their own writing on the computer. That process just gives me a headache—literally. It's too linear. I need to see the outline of my "quilt." So, I cut up paper copies of my articles, group them into piles, and move my piles around. I even take pictures of my table full of article clips to remind me of their arrangement. This process might be a bit old school, but it works for me. My recommendation is to do what works for you!

Research Method

Most popularly called the methodology (a word that literally means the study of method), this section is significant to different genres of the academic article—particularly those that use empirical research. If your description of the research method is detailed and accurate (or if it's available alternately through an online link to a detailed appendix), readers should be able to replicate the study and possibly reproduce your results. Similarly, they might want to start from your research to take the study of the topic to the next logical step according to your recommendations for future studies. This capability matters whether the research gathers quantitative or qualitative data because research that is one-off and not replicable may not be helpful to advancing knowledge in the discipline.

The methods section often isn't used in the humanities. Instead, humanist journals use the strategy of providing a clear, direct thesis that outlines the argument. The reasoning and proofs for the argument then follow. Sometimes British and other international humanist academics do write methods sections, but not all; typically, it isn't done in the United States. Graduate students often learn these distinctions in their methods courses.

When used, the methods section has several components determined by the type of article and study. Here are some of the most common elements that might appear in a methods section:

- Describe in detail how you studied your research question/s and/or tested your hypotheses.

- Clarify the reasons for your study approach, whether quantitative, qualitative, or mixed methods. Offer methodological theory for approaching your questions in a particular way.

- Describe the data collection processes. This section includes having received Institutional Review Board (IRB) permission to study human subjects, if applicable.

- Offer demographic data for the human populations studied (if applicable) although this subsection might be saved for the results section that comes next.

- Point to any appendixes with surveys, interview questions, and the like.

- Describe and explain reasons for choosing the selected theoretical constructs and/or taxonomies for data analysis. When possible and/or helpful, provide a sample data set or text that has been analyzed to demonstrate the analytical method. This also might be placed in an appendix.

- Acknowledge that this theoretical lens limits attention to particular aspects of the data. You also may describe the limitations to this methodological approach by establishing its boundaries and identifying what is and isn't part of the study.

ADVICE FROM A PUBLISHED WRITER

Everyone has a bias and an agenda. In one definition, a bias is a tendency to view an issue or concern from a particular perspective. Often, a bias is felt rather than reasoned; it's a personal judgment that sometimes may be illogical, irrational, or prejudicial. From a scientific perspective, bias is an assumption that a theory is true or false without any evidence or proof. Sometimes this bias may stem from ideological or political perspectives. Such bias can interfere with the scientific process, which requires reporting all data, even those that are negative or disproving of the theory or hypothesis. Researchers should objectively accept that a hypothesis is either correct or incorrect. An agenda typically is an ideological desire, plan, or program that underlies or grounds the author's message. Often, it's an unstated motive, which can cause readers to experience themselves as being led in a particular direction. When an author acknowledges a personal bias and agenda, readers can experience the message as more forthrightly presented, enabling them to consider their own biases and agendas consciously with regard to the argument.

Results

The organization of the results section varies based on the type of study. If the article is based on a scientific lab experiment, this section may provide some of the raw, uninterpreted data, or it may provide only statistically analyzed data. Most other types of studies require that you provide the analyzed data (using the analytical method described in the previous methods section) as the results. Likely, an article will provide only a portion of the data that is directly related to the thesis, or argument, that emerged from the results. Many studies—whether from the humanities, social sciences, or hard sciences—will yield sufficient data for more than one report of the study, which would be fashioned for different arguments, audiences, and journals.

For humanists, the results section may, in fact, simply be the analysis of the text or theory in question. This section narrates or explains the reasons for the argument and provides sufficient examples to clarify it for the audience.

Therefore, it's fair to say that the results section also tells a story of what the data actually say per the selected analytical method.

- Identify and analyze the study's population and/or other demographics, if not addressed in the methods section.

- Select a thematic, research question-based or hypothesis-based lens for organizing and describing the analyzed data. Let readers know how you are organizing the material. Where possible, make sure that the results are summarized either at the beginning of a subsection or at its end.

- As helpful, express key data using tables, figures, charts, and/or percentages or ratios. Other images may be useful particularly for humanities and social sciences articles. All such visuals must be identified and explained clearly and thoroughly in the text (keeping universal access in mind). Use the appropriate labeling and acknowledgement strategy per the selected research style (e.g., APA, MLA, Chicago, or others).

- Although a dissertation might address all the data from the entire study, be circumspect in an article about presenting the most important data for the research question/s or hypotheses. As discussed below, article length matters. It isn't necessary to recount every piece of data in one article. You may have more than one article to write from a single research study.

- Include a discussion that addresses whether and how the analyzed data provides answers to the research questions and/or hypotheses.

- This discussion also should synthesize what you've learned and what you want readers to take away as important from this study. It's often sub-headed as "discussion."

- Conclude this section with a brief summary of what has been learned.

> **TIPS & TRICKS**
>
> **Analyzing, Synthesizing, and Theorizing**
>
> **Analysis** is the taking apart of a problem, issue, or data set to look at it critically through a theoretical lens. **Synthesis** is the process of putting together the analyzed parts to create a new idea, theory, vision, or application. Just as combining polyester and cotton create a *synthetic* material, something quite different from both polyester and cotton alone, the synthesis of data findings and theory can create a new **theory** or application. Synthesis always happens before suggesting a new theory.

Conclusion

The concluding section of an academic article has many potential parts.

- Discuss the analyzed results if the work that wasn't included in the results section.

- Consider the implications of the findings for the research question/s and the needs of the scholarly discipline or field. Implications can extend to theory and/or practical applications.

- Address any limitations of the study's design by considering what the design misses or could have done better or differently.

- Describe potential future research that might strengthen, support, or extend what has been learned in this study.

- End with a brief one- or two-paragraph summary tying the major ends together.

References

The references section of an academic article is crucial to establishing your ethos or reliability as a researcher.

- Double check that every entry in the references matches an entry in the article proper *unless you're asked to provide a*

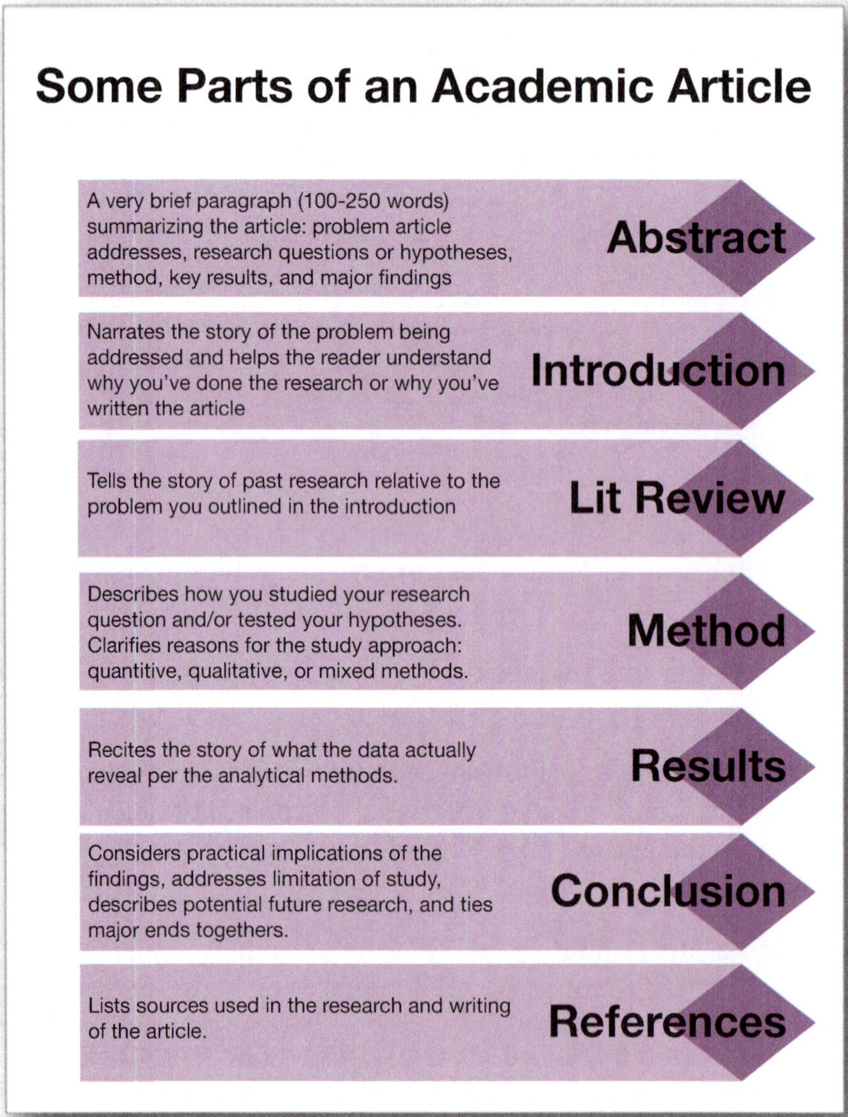

Some Parts of an Academic Article

Abstract — A very brief paragraph (100-250 words) summarizing the article: problem article addresses, research questions or hypotheses, method, key results, and major findings

Introduction — Narrates the story of the problem being addressed and helps the reader understand why you've done the research or why you've written the article

Lit Review — Tells the story of past research relative to the problem you outlined in the introduction

Method — Describes how you studied your research question and/or tested your hypotheses. Clarifies reasons for the study approach: quantitive, qualitative, or mixed methods.

Results — Recites the story of what the data actually reveal per the analytical methods.

Conclusion — Considers practical implications of the findings, addresses limitation of study, describes potential future research, and ties major ends togethers.

References — Lists sources used in the research and writing of the article.

Figure 3 - Some Parts of an Academic Article

bibliography in addition to cited references. Typically, then, you wouldn't list as a reference something you simply read if you didn't cite it internally (thus, *usefully*) in the document.

- Alphabetize the entry by last name for MLA, APA, and some other formats. References in scientific and other papers may be cited as endnotes or footnotes. Historians often use Chicago and tend to favor this approach. The protocol differs among the styles particular to different disciplines. Check your citation style manual for what to do if, for example, you cite more than one piece by any author.

- Unless you're asked otherwise at the point of submitting the final document, use the word processing program's automatic formatting function to apply a hanging indent; don't format these by using hard line returns and the space bar. If asked differently at the final submission of an accepted article, it's likely because of production requirements.

- Accurately use the style of the citation manual that the targeted journal uses or the one you've selected if there's an option.

- Be aware that journal editors may require a particular citation style but then adapt it for their purposes. For example, *Computers and Composition: An International Journal* uses APA style, but it requires authors to use the full name of cited scholars and not the initial-only format that APA describes. Attending to such details before initial submission removes a possible impediment to seeing the value of your work.

TIPS & TRICKS

It's good practice to save digital copies of all the articles you use in your research and written article. This practice will make it easier when you need to go back and check on a direct quote, page number, or a specific element of the citation.

Also save copies of all the drafts of your article—with different file names—each time you make major changes to it. There's nothing like doing hours of work and losing it with no hope of recovery after a computer error or human mistake.

Single and Coauthoring: The Good, Bad, and Ugly

Should you write alone or with a coauthor? When deciding to write an article, sometimes there's a choice about whether it should be singly authored or coauthored. We have participated in both types of writing and have published both individually and jointly authored pieces. Frankly, we like both ways.

Articles can begin and evolve either singly or collaboratively—and they can change even in mid-authorship. Nonetheless, the decision to write individually or collaboratively may well be dictated by your primary discipline. While the sciences have long favored collaboration, singly authored pieces once were—and still are—the standard for publication in many other disciplines. Examples include journals of literature and history although rhetoric and linguistics have moved away from strict adherence to this standard. Perhaps it was part of the old myth of the solitary scholar sitting in the ivory tower, scratching his or her head, chewing on the pen, and searching for words to express ingenious ideas. Perhaps it was because the promotion and tenure process favored individually authored pieces as demonstration of the author's research and scholarly abilities.

Certainly, when we started in academics, humanities-based disciplines frowned on coauthored pieces for promotion and tenure purposes; this position wasn't necessarily codified, although some promotion and tenure instructional material was written to urge scholars to publish individually. Indeed, it's still far more common in the humanities to see co-edited collections rather than coauthored books or articles. Talk to your department chair, dean, or mentor about your own situation. While a few coauthored pieces may be fine, if that's the entirety of your portfolio, it may hurt you for job search and promotion and tenure purposes.

TIPS & TRICKS

Check with your own promotion and tenure guide to better understand what's expected of you regarding authorship. If you're publishing simply for the purpose of writing and sharing something meaningful, however, feel free to decide how you work best and whether you want to publish singly or collaboratively.

Single Authoring

To author a piece individually, you need the motivation to get started and the self-discipline to see the process to the end. This motivation might stem from promotion and tenure needs or a desire to be hired to a particular institution or job. Ideally, that motivation also (or solely) stems from a genuine desire to say something of value to the discipline, something that no one else has said or could say.

The single author has sole responsibility for:

- Conducting and analyzing research (usually)
- Writing up the results, research, or analysis
- Determining the argument and developing it
- Brainstorming and organizing supporting material
- Targeting a publication venue
- Drafting and revising
- Getting a writing coach, colleagues, or mentors to provide feedback before submission
- Submitting the draft, including crafting an intriguing letter of submission
- Revising the reviewed article
- Completing any production phases for publication
- Revising for a new publication venue if the first one didn't work out

The benefits of writing alone include independent decision-making, complete focus on pleasing yourself and the publication's editor (i.e., no need to please a colleague), claiming single authorship (which, as we've said, still holds a high value in academe), ownership of the idea or argument (to the extent that one's field encourages or authorizes such ownership), and the freedom to claim the next steps in developing the idea.

There can be genuine pleasure in accomplishing a good article from the single-author perspective. For people who enjoy such work, writing alone can be both fun and satisfying. Yet, as we stress throughout this book, all authors—even the best ones—benefit from an outside reader or editor. So, hopefully, the process will never be entirely singular in that you'll always know you're writing for a real audience that expects others have read and commented on the piece

Coauthoring

The social sciences and hard sciences have a long, honored tradition of coauthoring papers for publication. In this tradition, the first and second authors are understood to have accomplished the most work on the research and resulting written piece, and those whose names follow have had some part in the study itself or in its writing. After the first couple of names, it's common to list the rest of the collaborators alphabetically, which in no way indicates how much work each individual did. Indeed, most scientific journals require that all coauthors sign some document (email or web-form) to actively affirm that they contributed to the research being published. The final author might be the most famous or prodigious, taking up a place of honor at the end.

Everyone understands that some research simply requires many people on the team to develop the study, collect data, analyze it, and write it up. It isn't unusual for a science-based graduate student to earn several publications on the basis of having worked on the advising professor's research. Sometimes, the novice scholar has done a great deal of work on the piece and gets a high place in the authorship queue; just as often, the novice is understood to be earning his or her *bona fides* and receives a lower place in the authorship order. For most novice scholars, such a publication is, indeed, a respectable start in the field.

Within the humanities, specific disciplines have begun to value the coauthored piece in the past few decades, and more such articles are being published than in the past. Coauthoring has gained respect possibly because social construction is one of the prevailing theories of how people learn and/or make knowledge. Edited books often are accomplished by a team of two or three editors.

Coauthoring a piece has the benefit of sharing the workload of research and writing, which can help to ensure a stronger research project and written product. Collaborating with a colleague can have other benefits in terms of enriching everyone's thinking by having someone to talk with about the ideas and knowledge that should emerge in the article. Collaboration can be downright fun, especially when two or more people who respect each other work together. Collaboration takes a special mindset, however, that can create an ongoing working relationship and possible friendship. Without that mindset, a relationship can fail to develop productively, and previously satisfying friendships may implode.

Successful collaboration requires an ability to cooperate, which often means negotiating a point, a written phrase, or even the inclusion of an entire idea. Whether there are two or five or more authors, in a fully cooperative setting, every author can be equal. Authors are human, however, and despite an ideal of no one author being substantially raised above the others in completing the article, often one person does do more work than the others. In fact, there is a tradition in some fields that the first author, because she is receiving top billing, does most of the work. The downside of such an approach is that those who are not first author may be underutilized or underappreciated—or they may choose to underwork.

Our take on this process is that if anyone whose name is on the document has a substantial responsibility toward it. To a reasonable degree, if there are three authors, each has 33⅓% of the billing and of the work responsibility. Whenever possible, all three should have a say in decision making; although, of course, having a team leader to guide the discussion is helpful. There is no perfect scenario, but we believe that in collaboration, everyone shares the work responsibility. If personal funds are required, for example, everyone participates equally. Well, that's the idea.

Practically speaking, collaborative teams may work such that, after the initial group discussion, one person takes on the first draft of the article. Then, the article might receive successive drafts, edits, and revisions as each coauthor takes a turn in the writing queue. Another way to work collaboratively is to assign each coauthor particular sections of the piece. The benefit to such a process might be that the parts are developed more quickly. However, at least one of the authors needs to review the entire piece and edit for a single voice. New technologies such as Google Docs, which enable multiple authors to work on a single document synchronously or asynchronously, are quite helpful to collaborative writing teams, allowing any number of writing strategies that get the draft done.

In any case, collaboration often requires a great deal of cooperation and negotiation, not only of topic and approach but also of process and a sense of when the article is complete.

Unfortunately, we've witnessed how collaboration can work out unfairly. Sometimes, rather than dividing up the work in equal ways, by default someone does the lion's share of the work. Usually, that person is or becomes the first author. Sometimes he resents doing all the work, and the relationship takes on the tone of unsuccessful college group projects (e.g., student writers complain that in their peer writing groups someone fails to show up to meetings, and someone else never submits her part on time, and one or more group members do all the work). In other professional collaboration scenarios, one writer may want to manage the whole project and give coauthors less responsibility, which is fine if that's what the team members signed up for. If not, it can lead to coauthors feeling as if they are less meaningful to the piece than the first author and may even lead to broken collegial relationships.

Team writing is a delicate process because it's as much about developing working relationships as it's about writing content and being published. Successful teams can be published again and again, and readers may begin to look for publications from them, eager to read their newest ideas. Unsuccessful teams may fail to achieve even one publication.

Successful team writers need to:

- Agree on the main idea of the research and article
- Jointly negotiate timelines and tasks, and then self-manage and meet those dates
- Learn how to write together, whether each takes a different part and then switches parts or writes simultaneously on one document
- Find a tone and voice that works for each author as part of the team, thus creating a group tone and voice

- Talk frequently enough by voice or email (remembering to be gentle and clear with each other), and write by distance or physically together depending on geographic distance

- Use collaborative revision and formatting word processing tools to their mutual advantage

- Respect each other's work

- Share the benefits and the challenges of the coauthorship

ADVICE FROM A PUBLISHED WRITER

I have successfully collaborated numerous times. Successful coauthoring requires knowing your own learning and writing style. It means making and meeting deadlines for each task. Nothing messes with a good working relationship more than disrespecting the set timelines as doing so gives the impression that you think your work—your life—is more important than that of the coauthors. "Co" means doing the work together. If that isn't your style, it's okay. Much of academe still favors scholars writing singly authored papers. That said, I've found coauthoring to be an extremely rewarding process.

Purpose

The purpose of any academic article has to be made clear to readers. Before that can happen, however, it must be clear to you, the writer. Sometimes the why of making an argument gets lost in the vast expanse of the how of writing. Indeed, in some disciplines, such as literature, the why is one of the most significant aspects of a piece, along with the so what? A major facet of most academic arguments are "Why does this matter?" and "What is the significance of this result/fact/thought/belief/practice?" In other words, it's important to express why you're writing this article and why the audience should care.

It may be helpful here to remind ourselves that there are various kinds of arguments.

Arguments that seek to **explain**, called *expository* arguments, tend to have several different purposes.

1. Explaining **why** something is as it is, its history, its theory or practice, and/or its state of being. In an expository argument that explains why, the purpose often is simply to inform readers, helping them to understand something that is. An example is a literature review section or article.

2. Explaining **how** to do something such that others can do it, too. In an expository argument that explains how, the purpose often is simply to educate readers on the process of doing something. An example is the research methods section of a paper or a practical applications or teaching strategy article.

3. **Reporting what happened** offers a new result or calculation to add to the data base of the scientific community. An example is a scientific publication revealing results of a study.

Arguments that seek to intellectually **convince** readers have a thesis with conviction, or changing people's minds, as their primary purpose. Rhetorically speaking, they use *logos*, or logic, as their primary argumentative appeal. The *ethos*, or known ethical character, of the writer/s also counts as an argumentative appeal. Beginning or novice authors must have especially strong logical support for their claims because their ethos won't be as powerful a rhetorical tool. We like to tell people that the goal of a conviction argument is to get readers to scratch their heads (figuratively, of course) and say to themselves, "Hmmm. I hadn't thought of it that way. Let me consider that claim." Such arguments don't always succeed in changing everyone's mind from a long-held way of thinking to this newer view, but they should be plausible and lead to further conversation and attention to the problem at hand. An example is the presentation of, and argument for, a new theory.

Arguments that seek to **persuade**, sometimes called *rhetorical arguments*, have a thesis with action as their core purpose. They must intellectually convince readers of the claim's truth and/or value. To this end, the logic must be strong and tied to the ethical character of the writer/s. To these argumentative appeals, we add pathos, or emotion, to move readers to an action. Appealing to readers' emotions of happiness, sadness, fear, anger, or love, for example, causes them to want to do something about how they feel. Persuasion typically asks readers to do something different, to make a specific change in their behavior, or to bring about change in the broader disciplinary community or societal sense. Examples of persuasive argument are to ask teachers to change their strategies or to politically appeal to readers to vote, write letters to their representatives, or sign their names to a position statement. Disciplinary organizations often make such persuasive appeals for their members to approach legislators or to ask for funding. A grant proposal, by the way, is a persuasive argument that asks the funding organization to choose to give money to the grant writers.

Article Structure

Journals and book collections typically have some kind of organizational pattern and information structure expected for submitted manuscripts. The closer the manuscript draft is to the expected structure, the greater the chance of getting a review, which in itself increases the chances of a positive review.

Take, for example, the following example structure requirements from the *Journal of Architectural and Planning Research (JAPR)* webpage.

> *Manuscripts:* Papers should range from 2,000-6,000 words in length. All papers submitted must be created in a word-processing program (such as Microsoft Word), double spaced, and formatted to print on 8.5" x 11" (or A4) size paper. Save the file in .rtf or .doc format.
>
> All papers should include on a first title page: (1) a brief title that is descriptive of the paper's contents; (2) the name/s, position/s, professional or academic affiliation/s, and email address/es of the author/s, as well as the full postal address for the corresponding author; and (3) a 45-character running title. The second page of the manuscript should include the paper's title and an approximately 200-word abstract that emphasizes the paper's contribution to the field and its practical architectural or planning implications.
>
> Source: http://japr.homestead.com/authinstrucC.html

These two paragraphs succinctly explain what the journal expects from a manuscript submission. When a journal sets out such clear and detailed structure information, you should follow them.

It's unusual for journals to lack guidelines, and most edited collection books have them, too. An edited collection might adhere to the publisher's own stylesheets if the editors are already working with a publisher. When guidelines aren't available, interpret what you can from published pieces in that journal or by the book editor/s or what can be found in particular publishers' books. For example, IGI Global, a publisher of thousands of edited book collections, uses the same book- and chapter-level structure strategies in nearly all of its publications. Some variations might emerge because of disciplinary expectations (such as scientific lab reports) or in the genre of the chapters as proposed by book editors. However, a standard usually exists. When it doesn't, before drafting an article or chapter that may be rejected or need to be completely reworked, confer with the editor/s. Email or call them; typically, they're happy to talk with authors and answer questions. It's entirely possible that they have a vision in mind that they haven't yet articulated, but that they need to express for the benefit of all the writers in the collection.

IEEE (Institute of Electrical and Electronics Engineers) magazines and journals share a standard structure. Journals published by Elsevier similarly share standard structures. Example 1 demonstrates IEEE structures as outlined in various hyperlinked nodes on their website. This example is provided to help you see what such guidance might look like.

Knowing Your Audience and Occasion

What you learned way back in first-year composition still applies. The audience for your writing matters a great deal. So, too, does the occasion for its publication when you can make it align with your topic, purpose, and audience. Here, we'll consider how to analyze the audience and the occasion for your argument.

Structuring the Article

> ### ✦ Preparing your manuscript
>
> Expand All | Collapse All
>
> **■ File requirements**
> IEEE publications accept Adobe PDF or Microsoft Word DOC file formats for initial submission. Check the requirements of your target publication by visiting the publication's homepage on IEEE Xplore, clicking the About tab, and then clicking on Additional Information. If your submission is accepted for publication then you will be asked to upload a final version of your paper before publication.
>
> **■ Graphics and multimedia**
> IEEE accepts PS, EPS, PDF, PNG, or TIF formats for graphics. Most graphics are published at one column width (3.5 inches or 21 picas wide) or two column width (7.16 inches or 43 picas wide). Use the IEEE Graphics Checker Tool to check your graphics before submission.
>
> IEEE accepts audio multimedia files in AIFF, AU, MIDI, MOV, MP3, RA, and WAV format. Video multimedia files may be in ASF, WMA, AVI, GIF, MPEG, or MOV format. Datasets are typically provided in compressed format in TAR.GZ, TAR.Z, HQX, SIT, or ZIP format.
>
> For more information, please consult Frequently Asked Questions About IEEE Author-Supplied Graphics and Multimedia (PDF, 120 KB) or contact the Graphics Help Desk at graphics@ieee.org.
>
> **■ Article templates**
> IEEE provides article templates for all IEEE journals in Word or LaTeX format. In addition to helping you format your manuscript, the templates also contain additional information on publishing with IEEE.
>
> **■ IEEE Collabratec™**
> IEEE Collabratec, a cloud-based hub for scholarly collaboration, features close integration of authoring and productivity tools with a networking community dedicated to technology professionals. Streamline the authoring process by taking advantage of offerings in IEEE Collabratec such as:
> - Virtual Private Groups to facilitate teamwork, share documents, and post messages to other group members
> - Seamless real-time authoring tools in Microsoft, Google, or LaTeX formats
> - Personal cloud-based document library with powerful document and reference management capabilities
> - Topical or geographic communities where users can participate in discussions, share links, and ask questions of other community members or IEEE staff; the IEEE AuthorLab, focusing specifically on IEEE periodical authors, is especially helpful
> - Connect and network with technology professionals around the globe
>
> **■ ORCID**
> All IEEE journals require an Open Researcher and Contributor ID (ORCID) for all authors. ORCID is a persistent unique identifier for researchers and functions similarly to an article's Digital Object Identifier (DOI). ORCIDs enable accurate attribution and improved discoverability of an author's published work. The author will need a registered ORCID in order to submit a manuscript or review a proof in an IEEE journal.
>
> Researchers can sign up for an ORCID for free via an easy registration process on orcid.org. Learn more at About ORCID or in the What is ORCID? video.
>
> **■ ScholarOne Manuscripts**
> ScholarOne Manuscripts, an online manuscript submission and management system, is used by most IEEE periodicals. The ScholarOne Manuscripts Author Guide (PDF, 2 MB) provides an overview of the system. Any specific questions during the submission or peer review process should be directed to the journal administrator.
>
> **■ Manuscript submission tips**
> Speed your manuscript through submission and peer review by following these manuscript submission tips.

Example 1 - IEEE Author Information

57

Audience

When you select the target journal, you're essentially selecting an audience, or readership, for your article.

People in your discipline probably have favorite journals they like to read. Some journals are the "must read" of any field; hence, they tend to be inundated with submissions and are harder to be published in. Other journals are specialized to one area of interest to the discipline. For example, while the *Linguistics Journal* is broadly focused, Language, *Linguistics, Literature—The South East Asian Journal of English Language Studies* would expect all article submissions to address issues pertinent to South East Asian scholars, educators, and students. While the *College Composition and Communication* journal addresses most issues relative to composition education, *Computers and Composition: An International Journal* was instituted to address the uses of digital technology in writing classrooms. Similarly, one can expect a different audience for the *Bulletin of the American Mathematical Society*, the *International Journal of Mathematics and Mathematical Sciences*, and the *International Journal of Number Theory*.

These diverse audiences present different challenges and benefits to authors. In a particularly specialized journal, for instance, authors have to share a certain depth of that specialized knowledge even to be considered. In more general journals, authors need both breadth and depth. For such journals, a specialized article might be considered too focused on a localized or side issue to accept it or that same article might be welcome because it broadens the knowledge of the readership. Understanding the journal's audience is all about reading that journal and determining—in an inexact process—whether your own thinking and knowledge seem to be a good fit. You also might read the letters to the editor, editorial, and Op-Ed sections. A more precise way to make such a determination is to write a brief (abstract-like) email to the journal editor to query whether the topic and approach of your article seems to address the journal's known readership.

- Having selected your audience, you must understand them. This means doing an audience analysis by asking the following questions:

- What kinds of scholars read this journal (or might purchase this book)? Are these the kinds of scholars you might gravitate toward at a conference or workshop? Would you purchase what they've written? Why or why not?

- What do they tend to care about? If they're educators, for example, they may have preferential leanings toward certain educational approaches (e.g., social construction, democratic education, and the like).

- What issues, theories, methodological approaches, and practical strategies do they seem to most appreciate? Can you realistically expect them to accept your claim and, if applicable, any proposed action you'll promote?

- What does this readership value in terms of scholarship, knowledge, education, political or other public policy?

- What are this audience's likely biases, and how might these biases be demonstrated in an agenda for change or resistance to it?

- What does this readership likely fear in relation to their discipline and its values or to the current local or global contexts?

- What do these readers need from scholarship? How can your research and its write-up help to meet these needs?

Specifically addressing the audience through such an analysis can go a long way toward making your article publishable in the selected academic journal or book. Additionally, audience analysis can help you if you also want to publish in more popular venues.

Occasion

One key to getting an academic article published is to submit it with an occasion in mind. There are times when a particular topic is more topical and therefore more appealing to the editor. For example, an article on political rhetoric is best received during or just after a major political campaign, with both you and the editor planning a year or so in advance so that publication is timely. If a biology journal has a special issue about DNA testing, that's the one to target for your article about DNA ancestry matching. Since the 55th anniversary of John F. Kennedy's assassination was in 2018, 2017 was the year to submit articles on his life, accomplishments, and assassination; this type of occasion-focused submission would have given editors time to plan for their 2018 journal issues. Similarly, as in the case of Kennedy, if previously secret documents are released to the public, as many were in 2017, the time is ripe to publish quickly using as many of those documents as possible.

Such plans for possible publication involve the Greek concept of *kairos*, or right timing, which for publication purposes suggests that when something is published at the right time, the audience may be broader and more ready for the message. Try to keep occasion in mind when developing your academic articles.

Word Count and Article Length

Does word count really matter to journal editors? Yes.

Editors of journals that print hard copy must watch the manuscript length—some via word count and others via page count. These journals pay the printer per page and may have a limit on pages they can use per journal issue or per annum. If per annum, editors might extend a single issue if there is a good reason for doing so, thereby shortening other issues. Otherwise, they strive to keep each issue to a particular length.

Therefore, it's imperative to pay attention to the journal's length requirement. If the journal offers a 5000 to 7500-word range, submitting an article with 9750 words, for example, reveals a lack of respect for the editor's needs and may result in the article not being reviewed. If in doubt, contact the editor with a brief description of the article and the word count of the drafted manuscript. Ask whether it's important to submit at the precise word count or whether a review might reveal areas that need to be cut or further developed. If your work is especially new or appealing, perhaps the editor would be willing to publish your piece in two parts. You won't know unless you ask.

AN EDITOR'S NOTE

The money for printing usually comes from membership subscriptions, university funding, and grants. Sometimes, however, it comes from the authors themselves. While, at one time, journals that charged author fees might have been considered taboo and of low quality, some journals with otherwise strong reputations have been pushed by their publishing agreements to ask authors for publication contributions. Be especially mindful of fees that may be attached to the manuscript length, as your agreement will require strict adherence.

Sometimes one must pay what is called a subvention fee even to publish with a journal or book publisher. Such fees are a partial subsidy charged when publishers may not reach more than a few hundred subscribers or sell up to 1000 books. They are designed to help the publication meet its costs. Your institution may be willing to pitch in with subvention fees, and the time to negotiate that assistance typically is when receiving a publication contract or when receiving or renewing an employment contract.

Subvention fees are particularly controversial in the humanities, where they're less common, and the controversy may be connected to a belief that if one must pay for the publication, it isn't a "real" publication. As higher education economics continue to shift, this presumption needs to be reconsidered in light of particular journals and publishers and the authors' and institutions' goals. As a part of such reconsideration, some scholars avidly recommend publishing in open-access venues that are free (usually online) both to authors and readers.

However, fees also may arise when a traditionally print, subscription-based publication also offers articles online as open-access to readers; in such cases, authors may have a choice whether to subsidize the open-access publication of their work as a way to underwrite the publisher's losses in subscription payments. Again, this decision comes down to the economics of journal publishing, which isn't inexpensive in any venue.

Interestingly, the uppermost limit of the prescribed length is one that academics tend to try to hit. We rarely see people writing article drafts that are substantially shorter than the limit. That may be because academic writers generally know to write with detail and have something they want to say. It also may be, however, a holdover from college days when professors expected them as students to meet particular lengths in their assignments. Because most journal editors must pay attention to length, it's a good idea to submit a briefer article if it actually is complete in terms of its message and thesis support. In other words, don't pad the manuscript!

Online journal editors may have a different concern about a manuscript's length. Although an online space might seem to be infinite and able to accommodate almost any article length, editors often have an internalized or even expressed article length in mind. Such preferences likely reflect a felt sense of article depth and breadth that seem ideal for that journal's mission and audience. Therefore, it's a good idea, once again, to check with the editor if the manuscript you want to submit is substantially shorter or longer than the journal's guidelines.

ADVICE FROM A PUBLISHED WRITER

I've been working with a coauthor on some articles based on our collaborative research. One small journal, which is printed in a newsletter or bulletin form, allows no more than 4000 words including the references. When using tables and/or charts, the space they require means further cutting word count. This extremely short length requires an exceptionally limited and targeted argument with no space for excess points or wordiness. Simultaneously, we're working on a much longer article targeted to a different audience for a print journal with a concurrent online presence; the page limit for this journal is up to 40 double-spaced pages of 12-point Times New Roman font, again with references included. These vastly different venues have required that we think flexibly about the argument and the most relevant points we want to make for the audience, as well as the depth of detailed support each argument requires.

Even if there are no guidelines regarding manuscript length for the online journal, please be fully aware of whether it publishes traditional texts or webtexts/hypertexts that make use of the unique functionality of the Internet. Webtexts and hypertexts enable internal hyperlinking as well as the use of still and video images, podcasts, audio files, and the like. Submitting the right kind of article will make all the difference in whether your piece is reviewed positively or even reviewed at all.

Finally, knowing the word or page count is a genuine benefit to the writer. The required or preferred article length can help you structure the article and determine the depth of detail and number of examples to provide.

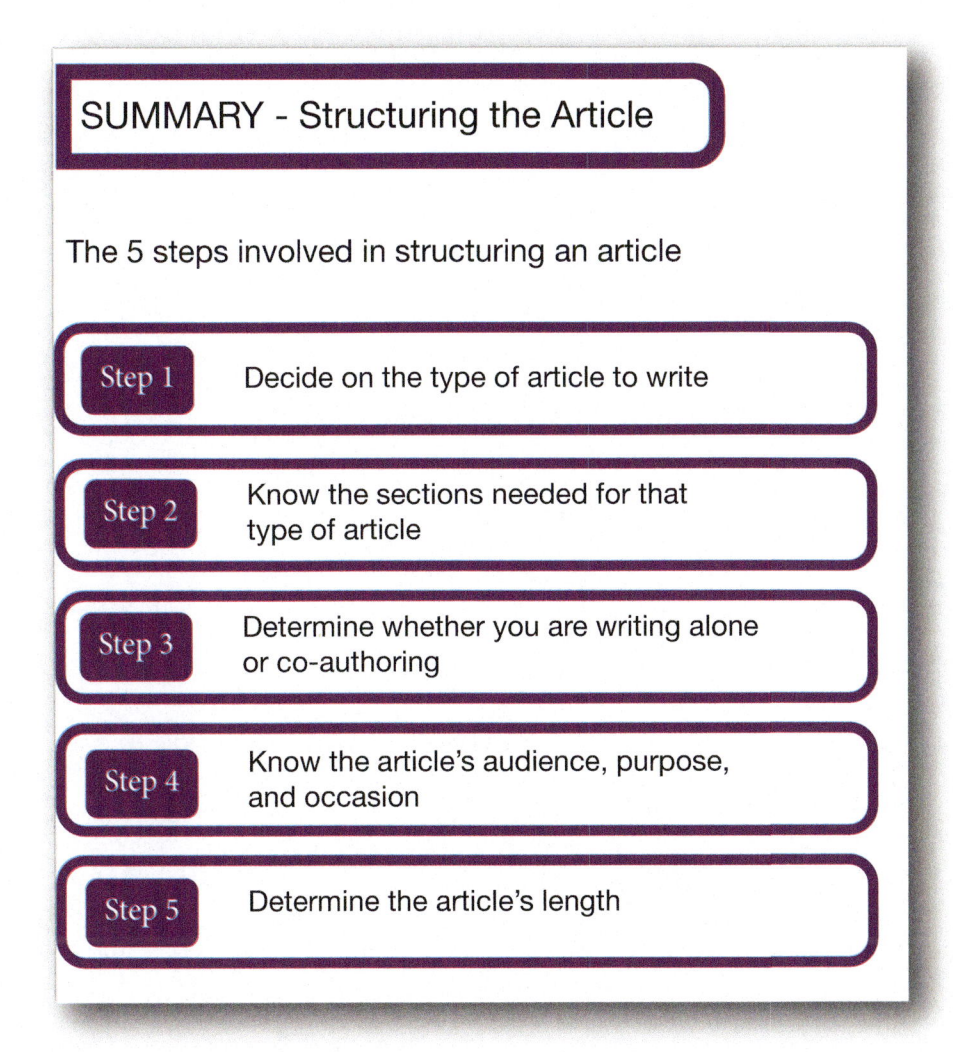

SUMMARY - Structuring the Article

The 5 steps involved in structuring an article

- **Step 1**: Decide on the type of article to write
- **Step 2**: Know the sections needed for that type of article
- **Step 3**: Determine whether you are writing alone or co-authoring
- **Step 4**: Know the article's audience, purpose, and occasion
- **Step 5**: Determine the article's length

Summary 2 - Structuring the Article

3

Revising & Editing

When you commit to writing an academic article of any form, you're committing to a lengthy and often painstaking process of drafting, revising, and editing. This process may require several cycles, and it may mean engaging with your manuscript for 30 to 50 or more hours. That said, a painstaking process doesn't have to be painful. This chapter shares some processes for writing, rewriting, and perfecting the academic article.

Drafting and Revising an Article

Drafting an article occurs as you first think of what to say, outline it, find your thesis, begin writing, and rewrite to strengthen the piece. The drafting process occurs differently for each writer, but people often try to write parts of the article (as described in Chapter 2) one at a time. However, if you're a person who has the full article in mind prior to writing, the process might be more of a beginning-to-end experience.

Drafting is a process of writing a series of increasingly more focused, complete, and sophisticated versions of the piece. This writing process is a progression from a collection of rough ideas to the final published piece. Think of these as zero, preliminary, presentation, and publication drafts, terms that reflect level of readiness for sharing with others.

- The **zero draft** can look a lot like a brainstorming outline. Ideas may not be in any particular order, they may not have any depth of detail yet, and they may be roughly focused. Generally speaking, a zero draft is a bit too messy and incomplete to show others, but it's a start.
- The **preliminary draft**, or *series of drafts* more commonly, includes revised versions of the article that circle in closer and closer to what it ultimately will be. Over time, you may write as many as 5 to 10 or more versions of the preliminary draft. The

- The **presentation draft** remains a draft, not necessarily a finished version. However, it's closer in appearance and substance to what you want to say to others. It's ready for someone's review and feedback. It's the one you send to colleagues and friends for their feedback, so you can edit and revise with an outside perspective *before* you submit it to the journal. The presentation draft, while not necessarily perfect, isn't embarrassing because it's solid.

- Eventually, all these drafts lead to a **publication draft**, a final, finished piece that's ready for the public's eyes. The article has undergone a transformation from the zero to the publication draft. It took hard work and focused layers of thinking and (re)writing to get here. A publication requires a final draft that has undergone significant attention and transformative work. This is the draft you will submit to the journal or edited book for review.

If you want to be published, expect the process *to be a process*, not a one- or two-shot deal that may have worked for a graduate school term paper. Developing writing for publication takes extensive hours of work. Eventually, you may become quite good at such writing and cut through the drafted versions to write something publication worthy more quickly. However, a new idea or line of thinking or subject matter

TIPS & TRICKS

Public, from the Latin word publicus, and publication, from the Latin publicatio have a similar root. Anything directed to the public relates to or affects the people as an organized community, which is distinguished by common interests and characteristics, as in the case of academe. A publication to such a community announces, proclaims, and otherwise communicates to the public involved. Our point is that a publication must be ready for the public's complete attention—hence, the hard work of the zero, preliminary, and presentation drafts leading to the publication itself.

may return even the most experienced of published authors back to beginning with a zero draft. That's because new ideas often cause writers to lose fluency while they're learning them and working out what they mean and how they matter.

The Layers of Revision and Editing

Revision

Revision and editing aren't the same thing even though they're often spoken of in the same way. Revision, as detailed below and summarized in Figure 4, typically means (re)viewing the text at a global level, as described above regarding preliminary drafts. It often means making more substantive changes to the content and structure of the article than you may have planned. When revising, look for the following types of issues:

- Is there a main idea or thesis evident? Can readers find and understand what that main idea is? Should it be moved to a more prominent section or paragraph? Should it be repeated in the same or different terms in another place or places in the piece?

- Are the paragraphs supportive of that thesis? Do any veer off to a connected yet different topic area? If so, perhaps those should be eliminated or summarized in a footnote as a point of interest.

- Are the paragraphs fully detailed? Do they have symmetry about them in terms of length? If one paragraph is noticeably short and the others are much longer, that difference may suggest that you're trying to emphasize what is in the shortest paragraph to catch readers' attention. However, if there's irregularity about length where one or two paragraphs are long and the rest are short, you may have excessive detail in the longer paragraphs or lack needed detail in the shorter ones.

- Is the piece organized in a comprehensible manner? Is it organized according to the major parts necessary for an article of a particular genre in your discipline (perhaps as outlined

67

in Chapter 2)? Within those selected parts, is it organized coherently according to chronology, importance, theme, or theory? In other words, organization is a global issue for the entire piece, and it's a local issue within subsections and paragraphs. Are there headings and subheadings to indicate the organization for readers? Are there sufficient transitions to guide readers?

- Does the piece reflect the specific style of the selected genre? Does it meet the style stipulations of the selected journal or book entry? By style, we mean everything from types of topics featured (if in doubt, query the editor about your idea), organizational structures, paragraph and sentence constructions, alphabetic text to multimodal feature ratio, tense choices, citation strategies, and the like.

Editing

When you're sure you've done the revision necessary to get your piece up to top presentation draft readiness, then look to editing. Poorly edited documents are turn-offs to journal and book editors who have more important things to do than to wade through poorly constructed sentences with misspellings and omitted words. To some degree, editing can be likened to proofreading in that the two processes are looking for similar issues. However, we'd prefer to slow down these final two processes and see them as successive steps.

Let's look at the editing process as that of making the perfect gift for someone. The gift of the writing itself matters as we don't want to disappoint the receivers, and we want those people—as our audience—to recognize that we've prepared the gift especially for their critical and experiential needs in mind. Such a process of perfecting the gift involves active managerial authority with creative or critical thinking to make or suggest meaning-based changes.

If the article's final draft is the gift, then editing is the act of putting the gift in a box that fits it well. Editing is reading for clarity and consistency. It involves such actions as addition, deletion, substitution, and reorganization of words, phrases, and sentences. It also involves:

- Writing the abstract, keywords, and author/s' biographies
- Rewriting any words, phrases, or sentences that would clarify potentially muddy or uncertain material
- Providing sufficient, useful transitions as signposts to aid readers
- Addressing sentence-level concerns
    - Eliminating unnecessary repetition
    - Adding necessary repetition for coherence
    - Searching for missed idea and thematic connections
    - Tightening sentences to eliminate unnecessary phrases and words
    - Matching tenses to selected genre and journal editorial style
    - Matching in-text citations to those found in the bibliography
- Checking and making needed changes to word count
- Checking the number of references allowed or needed
- Perfecting the citation usage in accordance with the preferred style
- Attending to stylistic issues specific to the journal as identified in author/submission guidelines
- Following formatting guidelines for figures and tables, to include moving, changing titles of, or adding text for charts, tables, and images
- Designating where and how webtexts are to be hyperlinked
- Indicating how and where such multimodal affordances as images, audio, and video are to be introduced, provided, and/or linked

In Chapter 2, we talked about the importance of word count. This issue is both a revision and editing concern. As Example 2 demonstrates, when an abstract is too long, editing for concision is the main goal. This draft abstract started at 132 words. However, the word allowance was 75-100 words. See how the abstract changed as it was revised for clarity and word count.

Layers of Revising, Editing, & Proofreading

Revising
Re-viewing and rewriting the text at a global level.

Editing
Reworking words, phrases, and sentences for clarity and consistency by adding, deleting, substituting, and reorganizing.

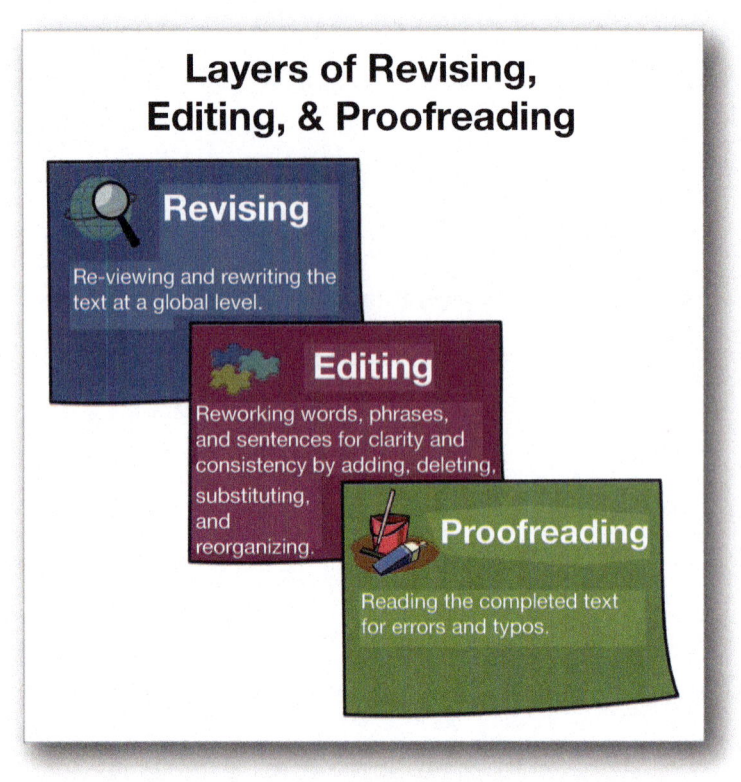

Proofreading
Reading the completed text for errors and typos.

Figure 4 - Layers of Revising, Editing, & Proofreading

In Example 2, the concision created by deleting, substituting, and rearranging words, phrases, and sentences is beneficial. It also involved adding active verbs and precise nouns to create more concrete and pointed statements. While deleting the final sentence does eliminate useful information, it's something that readers of the chapter easily can learn.

Abstract Moving Through the Revision Process

Draft (132 words):

This article addresses practical strategies for training teachers to teach multimodal composition in online courses. Specifically, trainers should focus on at least four skill sets: developing and scaffolding multimodal assignments; creating multimodal instructional tools; incorporating technology labs within the curriculum; and adopting and adapting the multimodal ePortfolio as a reflective document for showcasing student learning. Teachers particularly benefit from these skill sets, which enable them to guide students in acquiring such multimodal literacies as learning to design rhetorically effective multimodal projects for various audiences and purposes. The chapter offers theoretical and practical advice for trainers where the instruction will occur in online settings as well as the training itself. This advice also is useful for teachers of face-to-face (onsite) multimodal courses when using a robust Learning Management System (LMS) for student support.

Revision Process (changes identified):

- ~~strikethrough~~ = text deleted
- **purple font** = text added or moved

~~This article addresses~~ **Trainers need** practical strategies ~~for training teachers~~ **preparing educators** to teach multimodal composition in online courses. ~~Specifically, trainers should focus on at~~ **At** least four skill sets **are important**: developing and scaffolding multimodal assignments; creating multimodal instructional tools; incorporating technology labs within the curriculum; and adopting and adapting the multimodal ePortfolio as a **self**-reflective **capstone** document ~~for showcasing student learning~~. Teachers particularly benefit from these skill sets, which enable them to guide students in acquiring such multimodal literacies as learning to design rhetorically effective multimodal projects for various audiences and purposes. ~~The chapter offers~~ **We offer** theoretical and practical advice for trainers where **both** the **training and the** instruction will occur in online settings. ~~As well as the training itself. This advice also is useful for teachers of face-to-face (onsite) multimodal courses when using a robust Learning Management System (LMS) for student support.~~

Revised Abstract (99 words):

Trainers need practical strategies for preparing educators to teach multimodal composition in online courses. At least four skill sets are important: developing and scaffolding multimodal assignments; creating multimodal instructional tools; incorporating technology labs within the curriculum; and adopting and adapting the multimodal ePortfolio as a self-reflective capstone document. Teachers particularly benefit from these skill sets, which enable them to guide students in acquiring such multimodal literacies as learning to design rhetorically effective multimodal projects for various audiences and purposes. We offer theoretical and practical advice for trainers where both the training and the instruction will occur in online settings.

Example 2 - Abstract Moving Through Revision Process

AN EDITOR'S NOTE

Make a habit of using tracked changes (or the history feature of Google Docs), saving each draft separately rather than simply overwriting the same file when editing. Too many people overwrite the same file, choose not to use tracked changes to mark what they've edited, and then cut material they later may want to add back in. If you don't save earlier versions, the material is gone!

Proofreading

After editing comes proofreading, which some people call copyediting. Proofreading can be likened to wrapping the gift package, adding a pretty bow, and generally making it attractive to the recipient or audience. Although a gift can be offered unwrapped and without a box or a bow, it will be less interesting—compared to other, more attractive packages. Remember that there's strong competition with other academic writers for scant journal spaces. Your article needs to be competitive in every way; sloppy proofreading sends a message that's hard to overcome with a new iteration.

When the article's text is fixed, or stable, and won't change to any great degree, proofreading provides the final review of the package, the bow so to speak. For example, proofing includes checking for whether you've accurately used authors' first names where last names are needed or other incorrect uses of authors' names or titles. Proofreading also involves:

- Fixing typing errors and other such mistakes as
    - Spelling errors
    - Mechanics errors
- Running a spell check
- Standardizing text style
    - Fixing margins, headers, footers, and numbering
    - Setting appropriate font style and size

- Setting required and consistent line spacing
- Adding or deleting paragraph indentations or spacing per journal or book style
- Using the auto formatting features for paragraphing (tabs), block quotes (indent) and hanging indents (special indentation) to create perfect bibliographic entries

• Setting final hard page breaks, paying attention to widows and orphans

Proofreading is such an important final step to a publication draft, one that will go to an editor for initial review, that we suggest several ways of accomplishing it.

1. **Do it yourself**

    a. Print the document and read from the hard copy. Using a piece of paper to cover the text below your reading line, read it aloud to yourself, uncovering lines as you read. This process involves four of your senses: sight, hearing, speech, and touch—ensuring maximum attention to the words and their meaning.

    b. Pay attention to the potential for misreading what actually is on the page for what your eyes and mind believe ought to be on the page. Make written, hardcopy changes that improve the text in such cases.

    c. Return to the computer document to make the all the needed changes.

    d. Then, read aloud once more—perhaps from the computer screen this time.

    e. Spell check (even if you've already done it) to look for errors you may have introduced in the proofing process.

2. **Involve another person**

    a. Print two copies of the document, and—again using paper to uncover lines—read aloud to another person, who also is reading from a copy of the document. This process involves your four senses of sight, hearing, speech, and touch as well as the other reader's sight, hearing, and (possibly) touch. This proofing process helps to maximize the human senses attending to your writing.

b. Alternatively, have this other person proof for you by reading aloud while you listen and make written notations about needed or potential changes.

To find an additional, appropriate outside reader prior to submission, consider the following:

- Do you and a colleague or peer owe each other a favor, or do you work particularly well together? If so, you may be able to ask one another for a critical and/or proofing reading of the piece. Be sure to show appropriate gratitude and return the favor.

- Do you know a content or subject matter expert (commonly called an SME), or do you have a mentor in the field who has expressed an interest in reading your work? Consider carefully whether you should ask for this person's help, as she or he may be terribly busy. Show consideration, respect, and appropriate gratitude for any help you do receive. Acknowledge the help and pay attention to what you're told.

ADVICE FROM A PUBLISHED WRITER

Based on my experiences with European journals, don't take anything for granted—not even pesky words like "versus" and how it might be abbreviated as "vs" or even "v." My dear editor tells me "till" isn't even a word in English. Well, it's not unless you leave this country.

SUMMARY - Revising & Editing

Four types of drafts as you prepare an article for publication
1) Zero draft
2) Preliminary draft
3) Presentation draft
4) Publication draft

The layers of revision, editing, and proofreading.

Revising - re-viewing the text at a global level

Editing - reworking words, phrases, and sentences for clairty and consistency by adding, deleting, substituting and reorganizing

Proofreading - Conducting a final review to catch all spelling, grammatical, formatting, and style errors or issues.

Summary 3 - Revising & Editing

Submission & Review Process

Once upon a time, the way to submit a journal article was through the postal mail system. Doing so involved printing out the manuscript draft and sending as many as three or four copies to the editor. The extra copies meant that the editor didn't have to make copies to send to reviewers. All that changed more than 20 years ago, when sending a manuscript via a mailed data disc became popular, saving paper on the writer's side. Then, journal editors began to request article drafts by email as a rich text (rtf.), Word document (.doc or .docx), or PDF. Now, even that step is passé in some cases. Many journal editors now request article submission through a web-based portal where a file attachment is required. Understanding the steps involved in submitting an article is an important part of the publishing process.

Submitting Your Article

The first step if you submit your article by email or a web-based portal is to check the submission requirements found on the journal's website. For example, the *Journal of Architectural and Planning Research (JAPR)* provides the following instructions to writers:

> Manuscripts for papers and design and planning projects should be sent to the Editor-in-Chief, [John Smith], via email at japr@lockescience.com. Nearly all scholarly journals are now accepting manuscripts only by electronic means. However, if you absolutely cannot do this, please send us a brief fax at +1-[number] with your contact information, and we shall do our best to accommodate you. Please refer to the Manuscript Submission Checklist found here for complete instructions on submitting papers to *JAPR*.
>
> Source: http://japr.homestead.com/authinstrucC.html

These instructions reveal considerable flexibility on the editor's part as they enable some way to send the document other than through email or the web. In the JAPR's case, they request that authors save their files in the .rtf or .doc format. An .rtf file can be read by most word processors and retain most formatting. A .doc file, also is readable on most people's word processors, and it retains formatting.

Some journals require articles to be submitted to editors through an online portal, where files are uploaded. These can be a bit trickier as they typically require multiple files for uploading to the site, which may be programmed to compile the documents in a particular order. Additionally, they may require you to provide such information as a biography, keywords, and an abstract in selected textboxes. Often, these textboxes limit information by character or word count, so it's best to write the information first in a document and check the word count before copying the text into the appropriate box.

For example, *Computers & Composition* has such a web-based system, as do others published by the company Elsevier. Example 3 shows the checklist *Computers & Composition* provides writers to help them keep track of each item that needs to be submitted separately.

Check List for Authors
Required Submission Criteria

Order of Submission

The order of your new submission should be as follows:

1. Cover Letter
2. Conflict of Interest Forms
3. Manuscript File (should include title page, full manuscript body text, conflict of interest statement, references, and table and figure legends)
4. All Regular Tables (in order of citation within the manuscript text)
5. All Regular Figures (in order of citation within the manuscript text)
6. All Supplementary Materials
7. Highlights

Source: http://cdn.elsevier.com/promis_misc/gynor-checklist-november.pdf

---

Example 3 - ELSEVIER Submission Check List for Authors (Partial)

In the case of web submissions, it's best to have all files prepared prior to beginning the submission process, which will make the actual submission much easier and quicker.

Most journals use a double-blind process. In other words, the authors are unknown to reviewers and reviewers are unknown to authors. Because of this focus on anonymity, journal editors typically require that authors submit their pieces with a separate title page and file on which authors' names, addresses, phone numbers, and biography are found. Identifying author information should not be included anywhere else on the document. This means:

- Having no name, institution, or email address on the document.

- Employing "Author 1" and "Author 2" when self-referring in the manuscript.

- Using a filename that doesn't have name/place identifiers (e.g., "new_age_architecture.doc" rather than "rwarner_new_age.doc."

- Removing hidden data and personal information (i.e., metadata) by using the word processing program's document inspection function.

Let's add here that submitting a publication-ready draft for the first time to any journal editor can be scary. You've worked hard, but the question of how this piece will be received remains open. There's another way of looking at this next step, which is that at last you'll get the feedback you need and—hopefully—the validation of your thinking.

AN EDITOR'S NOTE

Perhaps a shift in thinking on why we publish might be useful. Try expanding your thinking on the objective of submitting a paper to a journal from an end game of publication (which becomes a happy by-product or a bonus) to getting access to feedback, support, and suggestions you normally wouldn't have access to. In this respect, peer review becomes more than people evaluating your work. It becomes an opportunity for colleagues to help you see your piece and your ideas from a different viewpoint.

Writing a First Letter/Email of Submission

Prepare a letter/email of submission for every manuscript submission. Such a message should be brief but pointed. Address it to the editor/s, whose name/s will be available online. If you're submitting the manuscript via email, this message may comprise the body of a formal introductory email.

In your message, provide the following types of information:

- A return postal mailing address with your institutional or home address, as well as email, phone, and other pertinent contact information

- Your background discipline or field and institutional affiliation, if any

- The proposed or tentative title of the manuscript

- Why you wrote the manuscript (i.e., What sparked your interest in this topic? Is this piece connected to a particular CFP for a special issue, for example?)

- Why you believe this manuscript fits the mission of this journal

- A brief description of the primary research question/s or thesis, the type/s of research conducted, a general sense of the data results, and what that means for your argument

- A polite closing to thank the editor/s for their time and attention

It also helps to state outright that you're looking forward to the feedback and to making any revisions that will strengthen the paper.

What Comes after Submission?

Congratulations! You've written and submitted a manuscript for a journal review. Breathe a sigh of relief and clean off your desk! The newly cleaned desk is a reminder of a task well completed.

Next comes the waiting for a response. Your first response might be an automated email acknowledgement of the manuscript's receipt. This message might be all you receive for a while.

Although it can seem like forever, an appropriate amount of time to expect before hearing back from a journal is between six weeks and four months. If it takes longer than that, connect with the editor.

That said, the editor has a multi-step job before getting back to the author:

> **Step 1: Personally review the text** to see whether it fits the journal's mission and style, as well as whether the subject and writing style shows the appropriate levels of sophistication and professionalism for that venue. If not, you'll likely receive a kind rejection letter that either invites you to try again (revise and resubmit) or offers advice as to other journals that might be more appropriate.
>
> **Step 2:** If the text passes the first stage review, the editor must **determine which reviewers will be the best fit** for the manuscript's subject matter.
>
> **Step 3:** If those reviewers are available, the editor will **send them the manuscript.** Usually, they have up to three or four months to conduct the review. Reviewers will read the piece and respond to specific questions provided by the editor.
>
> **Step 4: Follow up** with the reviewers if comments aren't returned on time.

Step 5: Seek new reviewers if the first one or two don't come through.

Step 6: Compile the reviews, make a publication decision, and write a letter to the author/s.

Step 7: Send the reviews to the author/s.

If you don't hear from the editor after two months, it's appropriate to write a brief email inquiring about the submission's status. Editors often will tell contributors what their timeline is, but it's perfectly acceptable to ask. After you hear back from the editor about the status, be as patient as possible in awaiting further word. It's the editor's job to usher the best pieces through the publication pipeline, so your respectful politeness will serve you well.

In the meantime, why not think about beginning another article?

TIPS & TRICKS

If you are ever tapped to review an article, try to turn around that review quickly, helping to alleviate another scholar's need to know how it's been received.

Editor and/or Reviewer Comments

For each writer's discipline, there are fairly clear expectations of an article whether it's a researched argument for theory, a report of completed research, or an exposition of research-driven teaching strategies. Whether that research is qualitative or quantitative depends on the research questions and the expectations of the field the author is attempting to address. Reviewers' comments typically follow the expectations of the discipline. When they don't, editors may remove those comments or convey that the author shouldn't weigh them as heavily.

When you do receive a response to the article submission, it's likely to have several parts.

TIPS & TRICKS

Reviewers are volunteering their own precious time to read and comment on your manuscript. They don't get paid for this time, and it takes away from their other work and from family and leisure. If your piece is a preliminary draft, argues an unclear or incoherent thesis, or has multiple errors, you're wasting their time. Their responses may be correspondingly curt or unhelpful. Peer reviewers can only work with what you give them. Give them quality!

First, there will be the editor's overarching comment, typically expressed as a letter. It usually includes a publication decision. The comments may be lengthy or short. For example, the editor will explain what he or she thinks, what the reviewers wanted or expressed, and the decision.

In response to one of Max's article submissions, for example, an editor wrote the following:

> Dear Max,
>
> I write regarding your submission of "Paper Title" to The ABC Journal of XYZ.
>
> Two blind reviews have been conducted by reviewers with research interests in the area of your study. They have made some helpful comments which are copied below. In some areas there is overlap in their comments which emphasizes for me that those are areas which need particular attention. The reviewers' comments also offer other points for you to consider.
>
> As it stands, the paper is not ready for publication in The ABC Journal of XYZ, but I would like to ask you to consider the reviewers' comments. If you feel able to revise your paper to address those comments, then I would be happy to receive the revised version.
>
> I attached a document containing a table. If you decide to revise your paper, please use the table to detail how you have addressed each comment in your revised version. This table will enable me to see how you have responded to the reviewers.
>
> I would be grateful if you could let me know by 8th February whether you intend to revise the paper.

The editor has provided a lot of important information in this short letter. First, he indicates that two reviewers who know Max's subject area have read and considered the piece. The use of the term *blind review* means that the readers didn't have Max's name or university information. The review actually is *double blind* because Max isn't given the reviewers' names or university affiliation either. Because a blind review is the gold standard, Max should understand that it was as fair as possible to his subject matter, leaving out any bias about himself as an author, which in his case includes his status as a dissertation—or novice academic—writer.

Second, the editor indicates that he finds the reviewers' comments to be "helpful"; Max should read this comment as the editor's decision to support the reviewers' views. To this end, the editor will want to see many or most of the suggestions addressed in revision. Editors rarely indicate they want all of the review response followed as the reviewers are providing guidance and not a fiat. Authors typically maintain choice both in what they revise and in how they do so. That said, wise authors pay careful attention to reviewers' feedback as they rewrite their manuscripts.

Third, the editor is clear that overlap in reviewers' comments means a weakness in the article that must be addressed. Max would do well not to ignore any overlapping guidance in the revision.

AN EDITOR'S NOTE

> Pulling an article when you've been given the opportunity to revise and resubmit often smacks of arrogance because it implies that you feel the editors and reviewers are wrong and your work is fine as is. An editor will usually tell you to address the reader's comments as much as possible, which means that if you disagree with a point or a suggestion and you can explain why and make a good case for it, the editor will let it stand. Reviewers have their own biases, too, and sometimes it's impossible to accommodate them—and editors know that. If the reviewer won't accept the paper without your changes, the editor will probably tell you that too.

The editor's fourth main point is simultaneously clear and potentially confusing. He states: "As it stands, the paper is not ready for publication in *The ABC Journal of XYZ*," which means that it cannot be published in its current state. That part is clear. The second part of the sentence, however, becomes fuzzier and demonstrates an academic attempt at politeness that can be confusing: "but I would like to ask you to consider the reviewers' comments. If you feel able to revise your paper to address those comments, then I would be happy to receive the revised version." The uses of the conditional "*would like to ask*" and "*if you feel able to revise*" the manuscript according to those comments lead to "*then I would be happy* to receive the revised version." This comment gives the author the authority to decide *not* to revise and resubmit, but it's misleading in its politeness. An experienced writer would know that *only if* the revisions are done will the editor review the revised piece. There's no middle ground to be debated.

The expectations of an editor for a piece usually are communicated in clear language, as described below and summarized in Figure 5:

- *Accepted as is*
- *Accepted with minor revision*
- *Revise and resubmit*
- *Not accepted* (Sometimes referred to as *Not appropriate for our readership*)

Accepted as is is a rare judgement from a journal editor. It means the writer has nailed the argument and has comprehensively and clearly supported it. Don't expect to see this response often in your academic life. If you do, however, celebrate because it should feel quite good to have created a strong manuscript on the first go-round.

Accepted with minor revision also is fairly rare, but it's easy to work with. Typically, such a judgment means that the revision requirements are straightforward and don't change the core argument. They may deal with tightening up a claim, adding or changing a few citations and sources, and making sentence-level fixes that the editor shouldn't have to address for you.

Revise and resubmit is the response you should hope for. It's a great response to receive. To be asked to revise and resubmit the piece clearly indicates that you're on the right track and have submitted the article draft at a point where it was ready to receive helpful peer feedback. Editors expect that if you are willing to revise, you'll pay close attention to the reviewers' comments in doing so. There's a good chance for publication with this journal in the future, although it isn't guaranteed.

Editor and/or Reviewer Comments

Accepeted As Is — Article accepted without any changes. The rarest response from a journal. Few articles are ever accepted as is.

Accepted with Minor Revision — Article accepted with only minor changes required. Also fairly rare from journal editor.

Revise and Resubmit — Article requires significant changes, but editor will review again after revisions. Most common response.

Not Accepted — Outright rejection. Time to rethink journal selection and rework entire manuscript.

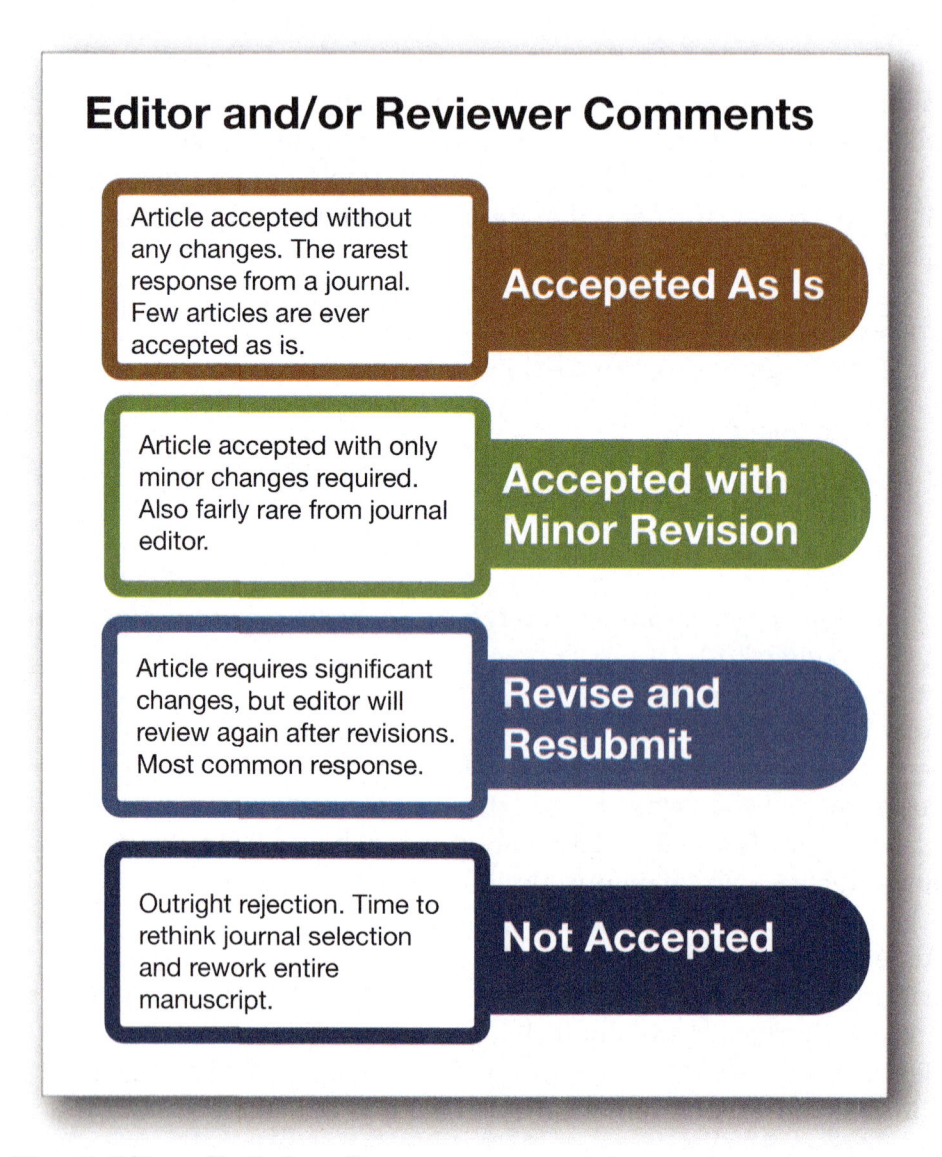

Figure 5 - Editor and/or Reviewer Comments

Not accepted or **not appropriate for our readership** may mean that you failed to choose the best journal for your argument. In that case, you may need to rethink the journal selection as discussed in Chapter 1 of this guide and give your article another go, so to speak. However, this judgement also may mean that you should return to the early writing stages and rethink the argument's premise and the evidence you're providing. In this situation, reviewers may not be as helpful with revision suggestions because the manuscript failed on too many levels to warrant their close attention or too greatly taxed their abilities to help you get on track.

In the letter to Max, the editor didn't give a clear statement of the manuscript's status, but we believe it can be interpreted to be *revise and resubmit*. If Max is interested in publishing in this journal, it's now time to read and interpret the reviewer comments.

Reading and Interpreting Editor and Reviewer Comments

A few final points are addressed in the editor's letter to Max. Editors typically want authors to respond in some written manner to each of the reviewer suggestions. This expectation means both revising the piece with those suggestions in mind and, in a separate document or letter, providing a written statement of what was done.

In Max's case, the editor provided both instruction and a table, shown in Example 4, as a mechanism for Max's responses to the feedback.

AN EDITOR'S NOTE

Editors often wish authors knew how to revise and respond to peer feedback more effectively. Even experienced authors let their feelings get hurt and then turn defensive and resist editorial and reviewer feedback. Good authors listen to and act on reviewer feedback. That's what humble and respectful authors do, and those are the authors whose work gets published over and over again. It's not a competition. Listen and learn. Assume your reviewers are right and figure out how to respond. When an editor shares comments from a reviewer, that generally means the editor agrees with them and wants the author to make the suggested revisions. Good authors listen, learn, and revise.

Author's Reaction to Reviewers' Comments [Original]

In order to facilitate the process, I would be grateful if you could use the following table to list how you have reacted to the reviewer's comments.

	Reviewers' Comment	Author's (Max's) Response
1	While examples of the greeting differences between Japanese and Americans were provided, a stronger intercultural communication reference would help, especially in the literature review and discussion of results sections.	This seems to contradict with the final comment about having more analysis and data described. 5000 words is not so many. I would hope to use less words than that even. I think I have just the right amount of intercultural interaction and if you really wanted to know how the actual data are analyzed, you should have been at the data sessions.
9	I'd be more interested to see how actual data are analyzed and more data are presented in the Result section, while many parts in the introduction and literature review can be cut off.	This seems to contradict with the earlier comment about having more intercultural interaction described. I added another table with a chart of the total data results. Some more discussion was added as to how the data was analyzed. But with only 5000 words or even less as it seems the whole paper needs to be tightened, you can read all about it in my dissertation!

Example 4 - Author's Reaction to Reviewers' Comments [Original]

The table the editor provided in Example 4 is a useful tool for offering response to the feedback. However, once again, in his attempt at politeness, this editor gave Max the wrong impression. In asking for "how you have reacted to the reviewer's comments," an experienced author would know that the editor wants a response that indicates what changes to the manuscript were made. Max, however, is new to the genre and misinterprets the editor's intention, thinking that he genuinely wants Max's literal reaction to the feedback. Max appears to be somewhat hurt and defensive about the reviewer's comments. As such, he writes his feelings about the feedback in an emotionally driven retort. He should have provided a more objective, intellectual response that outlined whether and how he was able to make the recommended changes to his article draft.

Addressing Editor and Reviewer Comments

On our advice, Max rewrote his comments to the editor and reviewers, as shown in Example 5. He reconsidered the content and tone based on the actual work he did in revising the piece. This example from the editor's requested table shows a more measured and far more professional response to the review, one that may inspire the editor to take his efforts seriously.

Although editors may not always use the most straightforward

Author's Reaction to Reviewers' Comments *[Revised]*

In order to facilitate the process I would be grateful if you could use the following table to list how you have reacted to the reviewer's comments.

	Reviewers' Comment	*Revised* Author's (Max's) Response
1	While examples of the greeting differences between Japanese and Americans were provided, a stronger intercultural communication reference would help, especially in the literature review and discussion of results sections.	**I have rewritten the piece to include two different examples of intercultural communication and two additional scholarly references. The revised literature review and discussion of results sections highlight these differences more strongly.**
9	I'd be more interested to see how actual data are analyzed and more data are presented in the Result section, while many parts in the introduction and literature review can be cut off.	**I appreciate your advice here. I added and explained a table regarding the data results as well as how the data was analyzed. I eliminated unnecessary material in the introduction and literature review to make space for this material and to stay within the 5000-word limit.**

Example 5 - Author's Reaction to Reviewers' Comments [Revised]

language to express their intentions, the "author's reaction to reviewer's comments" doesn't mean you should provide your literal reaction. Editors don't care whether you like the review; nor should they. They're in the business of providing the journal's audience with the best possible journal issue. Therefore, they care most about how you have revised the essay in response to the review.

AN EDITOR'S NOTE

Some editors look at part of their role as helping writers publish in their journal. These editors will have more extensive and instructional comments because they want their writers to be well aware of what revision is needed and how much work and effort they can expect.

Revising the Article

Take the editor's and reviewers' comments seriously and thoughtfully reconsider how you have structured the article and provided detail. For a strategy on how to do this, revisit the information provided in Chapter 3.

Revision literally means to re-see what you have written. If an editor is interested enough in your work to send you a review, particularly with a "revise and resubmit" invitation, then you must be sufficiently interested to really reconsider the problems they found. Every writer craves a reader. But, first, every writer needs an editor. The gift of an editor's response is the opinion of a seasoned, professional scholar's understanding of article writing, the profession's current conversation, and the focus and audience of that journal.

Therefore, try making the changes. Invest time in going through your own revision process for those revisions. Then, examine them carefully for the expectations expressed in the editor's letter. If necessary, revise again and again before resubmitting the piece.

Writing a Second Email/Letter of Submission

Once you've revised your manuscript, respond directly to the editor in a second email/letter of submission. Explain in detail how you revised in accordance with reviewer suggestions. If there are areas you chose not to revise, explain why. Often, that will be sufficient for the editor—provided your reasoning is good. Be sure to be appropriately respectful and grateful of the opportunity to revise and resubmit or to make minor changes for publication. Although it isn't necessary to fawn over the editor (that's actually insulting), be thoughtful of the time put into this process with you as well as for you. Therefore, make the message short, pointed, courteous, and friendly.

SUMMARY - Submission & Review Process

Submit Article
- Follow journal submission guidelines
- Write appropriate email/letter to editor

Responding to Editor's Comments

If editor classifies your article as "**Accept as is**," congratulations, your article is ready to move onto the publication stage.

If editor classifies your article as "**Accept with minor revisions**," make those revisions and then your article will be ready to move onto the publication stage.

If editor classifies your article as "**Revise and resubmit**," you need to go through the revision suggestions one by one and address each one and the revise the document as a whole.

If editor classifies your article as "**Not accepted**," consider options of an overhaul of focus/thesis/argument and/or find another journal for publication.

Summary 4 - Submission & Review Process

5

What's Next

You Were Published! What's Next?

Your article has been accepted, and the rejoicing begins. It's time to tell your friends, advisors, and supervisors the good news!

Proofs and Galleys

Your work isn't quite finished yet, however. You'll probably be asked to review proofs or galleys. This step usually happens several months before publication, but if the journal is online, you may be reviewing proofs days or weeks before the text goes live online. This review is both a courtesy from the journal and an opportunity to do a final proofread. At the galley proofing stage, there are a few considerations of which you should be aware.

First, you may receive an editable document on which you may make direct changes using track changes and/or comments. Or you may receive a locked document on which you may not make any changes; instead, you might have to make all suggested changes in a table using line and page numbers. This second method is a bit more tightly controlled than the first method. Additionally, you may be restricted as to how many changes you may make. This requirement is connected to the journal's own responsibility to the publisher to hold to a specific number of pages for the issue.

Second, because the type will be set, the kinds of revisions you are allowed will be local, few, and moderate. You won't be able to move chunks of text or to add or eliminate large amounts of text. Instead, your revisions likely will be limited to a word substitution, addition, or deletion; a change of tense; a correction of incorrect punctuation; and the like. If you made more changes that the editor accepted, those typesetting changes would cost the journal time and/or money.

Third, typically you'll be given a short turnaround window of two to five days. The editors deliberately offer brief turnarounds because they don't want extensive revision. They want authors to read carefully for the small issues you may change at this time, not to rethink the article's premise or primary argument. Any major revisions at this stage may change the article's position in the publication queue, boot it from the intended issue, or even cause the editor to refuse the article completely. It's critical, therefore, to respect the journal's timelines for returning the final document.

Fourth, don't be afraid to ask when the article is slated to be published or where it's in the queue. If this information isn't offered on the journal's webpage, don't be afraid to ask how to cite the article for your CV and whether you will be able to share hard copy or digital reprints.

Showing Appreciation

It's important to thank your editor for all the assistance offered throughout this process. Getting published is a challenging task given the many academics who want and need to publish. Editors work hard to bring an issue to publication, often for little to no compensation. They have a duty to the discipline and to the journal, as well as a duty to their own senses of integrity, to bring the best possible issue to the readership. You've had an important win, but your work was ushered through the publication process by the editor. Show your gratitude with a thoughtful letter/email of appreciation upon returning the galleys.

Who knows? You may be invited to write something for this journal in the future or to become a reviewer for other prospective journal authors. At any rate, you'll be remembered as a professional and considerate author to work with. Those attributes make you someone other editors will be eager to know because they talk among themselves.

Digital Access Publications Options

When a journal is published online or has an online edition, the journal may ask you whether you want to go the standard publication route where the article is only available to journal subscribers. Another option the journal may provide is to allow you to make your article freely available online at the point of publication for a fee that you agree to pay (and that you'll need to pay with a credit card prior to publication). This article publishing charge typically is a one-time fee that makes the article permanently freely available. While such a fee may not be cheap, it's required once only. Make your choice based both on your budget (and that of your department) and your needs for and/or beliefs about access to scholarship.

Sharing your Good News

Now that the article is published, it's time to share your good news. Since you probably wrote the article for professional purposes, start by listing the publication on your professional profiles. Here is a list of places to list your new publication.

- **CV:** The first place you need to add it is on your CV, both your electronic and print version.

- **Website, LinkedIn, and/or Academia.edu:** Add the publication to any professional profiles through a personal or department website, LinkedIn, or Academia.edu. If the article is freely available online through an open source like digital commons, include a link to the article.

- **Twitter, Facebook, or other social media:** Let your friends know of your publication and where they can find it.

You Didn't Get Published. What's Next?

If, after your best effort, you didn't get your article published in the journal you selected, you have several options. It could be that your article wasn't right for that journal and you need to move on to another one with the original piece intact. Or perhaps you may decide to do a substantial rewrite on the article and see whether a different journal is better suited for it. In either case, your initial rejection doesn't mean the article is without merit (or that you're an imposter or a bad scholar)/ It just means that in its present state, this manuscript won't be published in the original journal to which you submitted it. A rejection doesn't mean you should discard your article. It means you need to evaluate your choices and get back to work.

When Should You Move on to Another Journal?

If, after revising and resubmitting, you receive a second response from the original journal where the manuscript has been rejected or if the editor wants the same or even different revisions, think carefully about how much more time you want to put into the piece for this particular venue. Make the changes if doing so makes sense to you. However, if you object to the requested revisions because they somehow change the argument or leave out something significant, it's fine to call it a day and submit to a new journal.

ADVICE FROM A PUBLISHED WRITER

A colleague and I were writing an article together. We developed a set of tables to be used as takeaways for readers who conducted professional development workshops. The point of the tables was to provide trainers and trainees with material for the educational sessions they would share. For various reasons, the editors requested we eliminate one table and summarize it instead, leaving us with a dilemma. We genuinely believed that readers would benefit from having both tables and that removing one would limit the article's benefits for readers. As a result, we politely declined to remove the table in question and respectfully offered to withdraw the piece. It was then up to the editors to determine the next step of whether to compromise or to let the piece go. Ultimately, after negotiating the issue with the editors, we decided to withdraw the piece and move to a new publication venue. We think we communicated this appropriately with the editors as their email back to us was friendly as well as professional.

However, an offer to withdraw a piece should be carefully considered because academe is like a small town, and people talk. Be certain that you're ready to stand by such an action and that you have other ideas for a publication venue. As one might say in the military, don't fall on your sword for a small problem. To this end, always be polite and courteous even if the correspondence makes you angry. If a compromise is offered, consider it carefully before moving forward. Like bones, once professional relationships are fractured, they don't heal without scars.

From Rejection to (Re)Submission

If your manuscript has been outright rejected, it may be possible to resubmit it if the argument or its writing is reconceived and revised. Therefore, it's helpful to directly ask the editor whether you're welcome to submit a substantially changed draft and when it would be welcomed. If it would be welcome and since you've already established a working relationship with this editor, you may choose to heavily reconceptualize the piece.

> **ADVICE FROM A PUBLISHED WRITER**
>
> Years ago, I received a "revise and resubmit" on one of my manuscripts; I didn't have time then to revise, so I put the draft away and forgot about it. It sat in my file drawer for 20 years! One day, I pulled it out again and reread both the article and the editor's revision advice. Now understanding the changes the editor needed to see, I found a coauthor who could help shore up the argument's literary details to support my own rhetorical analysis. The piece was easily revised and published—in the originally targeted journal—within one calendar year. I'm not recommending waiting 20 years (one to six months likely will do), but give yourself some time and space to look at the piece objectively. Time away from an article draft never hurts. I'm the perfect example.

I'm not recommending waiting 20 years (one to six months likely will do), but give yourself some time and thinking space to look at the piece objectively. Time away from an article draft never hurts. I'm the perfect example.

However, if you think the piece might be accepted as is with another journal, moving on to a new venue might be the best move. How can you make that decision? Ask a colleague who is well published in your field to read the piece and the editor's guidance. If the colleague agrees that the editor is asking too much or suggests that the selected journal is the wrong venue for this piece, it's time to find a different journal. To this end:

- **Rethink your article.** It's not perfect—not even if your colleague agreed with your general plan. What can you change to make it better while keeping the main argument?

97

- **Put it away for a while.** Writers often benefit from time away from a manuscript. Depending on your time frame for a desire publication, put it away for a minimum of a week to a month. If you can go longer without looking at it, try to do that.
- **Revise the piece as needed.**
- Follow the steps in Chapter 1 for **finding a new journal.**

Last Words

We end with this encouragement. Although there's a good deal of competition for journal space, it's entirely possible to be published. You can think well and research, or you wouldn't be an academic.

Remember, if you're struggling on your own for whatever reason—a learning challenge, time restrictions, writer's block, writing in English as a multilingual scholar, or just novice uncertainty—help exists. In some disciplines, there are scholarly publication courses that do help graduate students and new PhD holders learn how to publish by going through the process of revising existing work. Additionally, it's okay to get a writing coach to help you. Make sure it's a published academic writer who knows the ropes from experience. Also, be sure to find someone who will teach you what you need to learn, so you can become more and more of an independent writer.

Gather up your good ideas and give the article writing another try because you can do this.

SUMMARY - What's Next

Article Accepted

- Review proofs or galleys
- Write thank you note to editor
- Decide on digital access options
- Share your good news by listing on CV, posting on social media, and emailing friends and colleagues

Article Rejected

- Find another journal and then carefully review manuscript based on journal's focus and audience and do a rewrite as necessary
- Query whether editor is willing to review a fully revised submission. If the editor agrees, then do a substantial revision and resubmit.

Summary 5 - What's Next

Acknowledgements

We thank Stefan Battle, Kristine Blair, Michael Greer, Barbara L'Eplattenier, Yuri Levin-Schwartz, Allena Opper, Nadia Schwartz, Larissa (Kat) Tracy, Gene Warner, and B. Bricklin Zeff for their comments, inspiration, and counsel.

About the Authors

Beth L. Hewett, Ph.D.

beth.hewett@gmail.com

beth@defendandpublish.com

Beth Hewett, a university-level writing and rhetoric teacher for more than 30 years, is an author and educational consultant in dissertation writing, publishing, and online writing instruction. Beth has authored and coauthored dozens of books and articles including: *Teaching Writing in the Twenty-first Century* (MLA, 2021), *Administering Writing Programs in the Twenty-first Century* (MLA, 2021), *Reading to Learn and Writing to Teach: Literacy Strategies for Online Writing Instruction* (Bedford, 2015), *Foundational Practices for OWI* (Parlor Press, 2015), *The Online Writing Conference: A Guide for Teachers and Tutors* (Bedford, 2015; Heinemann, 2010), *Virtual Collaborative Writing in the Workplace: Computer-Mediated Communication Technologies and Processes* (IGI Global, 2010), *Technology and English Studies: Innovative Career Paths* (Lawrence Erlbaum, 2006), and *Preparing Educators for Online Writing Instruction: Principles and Processes* (NCTE, 2004). Beth founded Defend & Publish, a boutique writing coaching company for adult academic writers of theses, dissertations, articles, and books. She was the founding president of the Global Society for Online Literacy Education (GSOLE), prior Chair of the CCCC Committee for Effective Practices in Online Writing Instruction, and prior co-editor of *Kairos: A Journal of Rhetoric, Technology, and Pedagogy.* She was the initial developer of the online writing program at Smarthinking, Inc. and redeveloped the writing program for TutorVista, leading to its purchase by Pearson, Inc. Beth also works as a trained and certified bereavement support coach and facilitator trainer.

Robbin Z. Warner, Ph.D.

robbin.warner@gmail.com

robbin@defendandpublish.com

Robbin Zeff Warner holds a Ph.D. in Folklore and American Studies from Indiana University and a B.A. in Anthropology from Berkeley. She has a long background with technology and writing. Her interest in the teaching of writing started through her involvement with the National Writing Project in 1993. Over the past 20 years she has taught writing at universities, summer writing workshops, and training academies. She has led writing seminars and developed online writing courses and online writing and research resources for universities, business, and government agencies. Her interest in online technology was launched when she wrote the landmark book *The Nonprofit Guide to the Internet* in 1996 when there were so few nonprofits online one could actually count them. This book initiated a series of books on Internet use for the nonprofit community by John Wiley & Sons. She then moved into Internet advertising and not only wrote the first book on online advertising back in 1997 (*Advertising on the Internet*), which was eventually translated into 6 languages, but ran the 10-city "Advertising & Marketing on the Internet" training conference series. Robbin is the author of 6 books and dozens of book chapters and articles. She has also published restaurant and chocolate shop reviews, written speeches and presentations for government officials and business executives, and developed research reports for businesses, agencies, and think tanks. In addition, Robbin is a trained chocolatier.